DAY FOR NIGHT

François Truffaut

DAY FOR night

Translated by Sam Flores

Grove Press, Inc., New York

Contents

Foreword

CINEMA IN ACTION

In July 1971 I found myself in a state of exhaustion, both mental and physical. I had just finished shooting *Two English Girls* ("Les Deux Anglaises et le Continent") and the sadness of the film had affected me. So, since my children were vacationing on the Riviera, I decided to have all the processed film sent down to Nice, where I could work on the editing in the more relaxed atmosphere of the Victorine Studios.

Every morning, while crossing the lot, I would pass a huge outdoor set that an American production company had constructed several years before for *The Madwoman of Chaillot*. The set consisted of ten or so false building fronts, a large café terrace, a fountain, a subway entrance, and a flight of stone steps connecting two street levels that would have looked quite at home in Montmartre. This immense set appeared already much the worse for wear, having been seriously damaged by the wind and rain storms that sweep down over the Riviera from the Alps during the winter months. I wondered why it had not been torn down. When I checked, I learned that the only reason it still stood there in all its faded grandeur was that demolishing it would have cost the studio too much money.

Intrigued by the sight, I began taking a different route to my destination each day, in order to view the square from as many angles as possible. The more I looked, the more interesting the set grew. In fact, it soon appeared most beautiful of all when viewed "wrong side out." It was then, I think, the idea hit me. A desire which had been playing around vaguely in the back of my mind for many years suddenly became crystallized: I would shoot a film about shooting a film—*a movie about film-making.*[1]

With this thought in mind, I began spending much of my free time visiting the many various buildings on the Victorine lot, which until now had never interested me all that much. I roamed around the production offices, rummaged within the empty dressing rooms, visited the various soundstages and auditoriums and screening rooms.

Already I had decided that if my story could take place entirely within this studio, I would have "unity of place" without even half trying. "Unity of time" resulted automatically, of course, given the premise of the shooting of a movie from the first day on the set until that final moment when the cast and crew disband. These two unities led, *a fortiori,* to the Aristotelian "unity of action" as well. In order to remain true to such a concept, I knew I would have to cast aside all material relating to the preparation of a film before the actual shooting starts. But that was all right too, I decided. Especially since Fellini in his 8½ had already treated (and, to my mind, exhausted) the subject. Furthermore, in order to retain that "unity of action," I would not concern myself with anything (editing, post-dubbing, the film's première, etc.) that occurred after the actual shooting ended.

Yet, even as I decided all this, I was not naïve enough to think my idea an entirely original one. I remembered quite a few movies on the same subject. And I liked all of them, or just about, my preferences ranging from Marcel Pagnol's *Le Schpountz*[2] to Vincente Minelli's *The Bad and the Beautiful* and Stanley Donen's *Singin' in the Rain.*

---

1. In English in the original.

2. *Le Schpountz* (1938), never generally released in the U.S., is the story of a country yokel (Fernandel) who considers himself a great actor and is taken to Paris by a film company as a cruel joke. He stars in what he thinks to be a great tragic role, but which is, of course, a farce. He becomes a comic star—and almost dies of a broken heart. As for the title, Pagnol defines *schpountz* as "a movie nut . . . once he gets it into his head he looks like some famous actor, he'll believe it all his life. You can pull any trick on him. He'll never realize he's being made a fool of. You come across these pathetic characters all the time in the picture business."—*Trans.*

FOREWORD
... ix

As a filmmaker, I have always been torn, on the one hand, by
my hatred for the documentary ("the most false genre in all
moviemaking," Jean Renoir rightly terms it) and, on the other,
by my desire to use as the basis for all my scripts something which
began as real-life fact (although, until now, I have limited myself
to one "didactic fiction," *The Wild Child*). This time I decided to
construct, using as its starting point a film in progress, a *fictional*
story which would, at the same time, furnish a maximum of
factual information. I would not tell *all* the truth about shooting
a film. That would be impossible. But I would tell *only true
things:* events which had happened to me while making other
films, or which had happened to other filmmakers I knew. Each
character in my script would therefore have to be shown in a
double aspect: in his professional life on the set, and somehow
in his private life as well. As is usual in such cases, many of
these characters would have some secret unknown to the others.
The movie itself being shot would be the equivalent of the cattle
trek from Texas to Missouri in Howard Hawks' beautiful film,
Red River. My movie would also consist of a long crossing, a
difficult journey; and at the end of this trek a real *goal* would also
be attained.

To devise such a scenario, working with my collaborators
Suzanne Schiffman and Jean-Louis Richard,[1] I decided very
quickly we would have to invent a subject for our "film within
a film." The three of us rejected from the outset the solution of
leaving this element purposely vague, as that seemed too easy and
yet too intellectual a cop-out. We had no desire to get cheap
effects by causing confusion in our audience's mind between the
scenes of real life (the day-to-day chronicle of shooting a film)
and the scenes of fiction (those within our "film within the film").
No, we decided: the two films must remain separate throughout.

---

1. Suzanne Schiffman was script girl on *Shoot the Piano Player* in
1960. She has worked with Truffaut ever since, although also serving
as script girl for Godard on such films as *My Life to Live* (1962) and
One or Two Things I Know About Her (1966).

Jean-Louis Richard appeared as a performer in *Jules and Jim*. In
collaboration with Truffaut, he wrote the scenarios for *Soft Skin*,
Fahrenheit 451, and *The Bride Wore Black.—Trans.*

Therefore, the plot of our "film within a film" must be a simple one, especially since we would be showing only excerpts—and these, for the most part, highly dramatic, in order to contrast with the lighter tone I wished to impart to the chronicle of day-to-day shooting. Almost at once, we three decided to use for our factual basis a news item that had gotten a great deal of play in the British press some years before: the elopement of a middle-aged man with his young daughter-in-law. This story, which we christened *Meet Pamela*, would operate on various levels, all of them appropriate to our larger film: the conflict of two couples, of two generations, the dramatic action held together by a strong central situation. Perhaps most important of all, no matter what segment of *Meet Pamela* we showed (from the period of rehearsals through the actual filming to the viewing of the rushes) the audience would have little trouble in situating that particular moment within the totality of the story. Knowing this to be true, we suddenly felt much freer in our approach: for now we would not even have to present the sequences of *Meet Pamela* in chronological order, and could thereby preserve the "jigsaw puzzle" aspect of most shootings.

As for the chronology of the day-to-day filming, the scenario would consist of a résumé or recapitulation of all the various troubles that can plague a movie production. We decided we wanted to show a difficult shooting—but not an exceptional one. With this in mind, we created ten or so characters, being careful not to place them in any established pecking order. For example, right from the start, we gave the roles of the script girl and the prop man the same importance as the stars of our "film within a film."

In a more personal sense, another aspect of filmmaking seemed equally important to me. I wanted to make a French film, and an exclusively French film. Yet, for all that, I also wanted my audience to feel quite strongly the presence of Hollywood, that city (or state of mind) which has so profoundly influenced filmmaking everywhere. This became possible by entrusting one of the main roles to a young English actress who, although she speaks French quite well, is nonetheless known primarily for her Hollywood films: Jacqueline Bisset. To strengthen the Hollywood influence we then brought in a French matinee idol who had made the most important part of his career in American studios: Jean-Pierre Aumont. The character of an Italian actress who has enjoyed an international career, as played by Valentina Cortese, added still another desired element: cosmopolitanism.

Considering the complicated nature of all of the above, you might very well ask why I was so stubbornly concerned with making a movie about moviemaking. To answer that question I'll have to go back twelve years, when I was in Alsace shooting *Jules and Jim*.

One day I was setting up a scene, giving last-minute whispered instructions to the three actors involved, Jeanne Moreau, Oskar Werner, and Henri Serre. The time had come to get on to what we call "a serious rehearsal." I asked the two men to settle themselves on either side of a table and begin playing dominoes while Jeanne Moreau, hovering above them, a tiny stick in her hand, would deliver the line in the script: "Isn't there anyone here who'll scratch my back for me?"

At that moment, suddenly rushing into the camera range, came our prop man. So moved had he been by the reality of the actress's question that he had leapt forward unthinkingly to scratch her back for her. Naturally enough, everyone on the set collapsed hysterically; and when work was finally resumed, we all went at it with lighter hearts. For if it is always a good thing to laugh in real life, I can assure you it is even more essential while shooting a film!

During every filming there occur many such incidents. Not all of them are funny; sometimes they are simply bizarre and on occasion terribly cruel. Yet, no matter what, by their crude power they always contrast with the rather banal quality of the scene being shot. At such moments (for example, when at least two assistants are necessary to crouch on either side of a bed to hold in place the sheets being tossed about by a couple of actors mimicking the sexual act) a director is forced to admit that filming "the film of the film" would prove more amusing and certainly more vital than filming THE film.

Anyone who has ever visited a movie set for a few hours comes away with a feeling of malaise, which is caused by experiencing too much and yet understanding so little of what is happening. Arriving on the set with the hope of at last having all his questions answered, the visitor leaves dissatisfied. Such an emotion is quite understandable. That is why Jean-Louis Richard, Suzanne Schiffman, and I discussed this malaise a great deal when constructing our scenario of *Day for Night*.

To combat such a feeling, we tried, as much as possible, to make of each spectator of our film an observer on the set as well. An apprentice, if you will; one who will observe all that goes on for seven weeks' time (our fictional length) during one hour and fifty-five minutes (the actual running length).

At least a hundred times during the shooting I was asked, "But aren't you afraid of 'demystifying' (*demyth*ifying, one might almost say!) a craft you love so much?" I answered each time with a question of my own: An aviator can easily explain all he knows about piloting a plane—and yet will he ever succeed in 'demystifying' the intoxicating rapture of flying? Moviemaking is a marvelous business, a wonderful craft. If anyone still needs proof of that, let him consider how of all those who have the good fortune to work in films not one ever wishes to do anything else! You may have heard of the great circus impresario who, having gone bankrupt, ended up taking care of an acrobatic elephant who continually kicked him in the ass and who daily pissed in his face. One of the impresario's old friends, shocked at seeing the man fallen so low, berated him: "You have a university degree and there's nothing you don't know about accounting! Why don't you get yourself a wonderful position in business administration?" To which the impresario answered: "What? And leave show business?"

Day for Night revolves around one central question: "Are films superior to life?" It gives no definite answer. For there can be none. No more than there can be to that other equally persistent question: "Are books superior to films?" One might just as well ask a child which parent he prefers! Sometimes I receive in the mail theses (*written*) concerning my work (*filmed*). These students often point out to me how I insist upon inserting writing and the written word in all of my films. For example, it is through reading such and such a book that one of my characters first perceives that, etc., etc. Or it is in writing a letter that another of my characters sets in motion this or that action which leads to, etc., etc. Someone even wrote me once that if the apparent subject of *The Wild Child* is the attempt of Doctor Itard to educate young Victor of Aveyron, its *real* subject, one which I filmed without even realizing it, is the story of a film director who is writing a book by keeping a daily journal. This idea bothered me a great deal when I thought about it—perhaps because I saw some truth in it.

To the many questions the public might possibly ask along the lines of, "How do you go about shooting a movie?" I have tried, in *Day for Night*, to give some answers: visual ones, of course, the only kind possible in a visual medium. For all that, *Day for Night* has now become a book as well: Film-books, book-films—such have been and continue to be the daily round of my life. My twin love of books and films caused me to make *Jules and Jim*, as an homage to a particular book; and, five years later, *Fahrenheit 451*, which embraces *all* books.

By publishing in written form the script of *Day for Night*, which is in some ways the most "cinematic" of all my seventeen films,[1] I trust that once again my twin universes of books and movies will mix and intermingle, becoming completely entangled —and, in so doing, again make love with each other.

FRANÇOIS TRUFFAUT
October, 1973

---

1. *Une Visite* (1955); *Les Mistons* ("The Mischief Makers," 1957); *Une Histoire d'Eau* ("A Story of Water," 1958); *Les Quatres Cents Coups* ("The 400 Blows," 1959); *Tirez sur le Pianiste* ("Shoot the Piano Player," 1960); *Jules et Jim* (1961); *Antoine et Colette* (episode in *Love at Twenty*, 1962); *La Peau Douce* ("Soft Skin," 1964); *Fahrenheit 451* (1966); *La Mariée était en noir* ("The Bride Wore Black," 1967); *Baisers Volés* ("Stolen Kisses," 1968); *La Sirène du Mississippi* ("Mississippi Mermaid," 1969); *L'Enfant Sauvage* ("The Wild Child," 1969); *Domicile Conjugal* ("Bed and Board," 1970); *Les Deux Anglaises et le Continent* ("Two English Girls," 1971); *Une Belle Fille Comme Moi* ("Such a Gorgeous Kid Like Me," 1972); and *La Nuit Américaine* ("Day for Night," 1973).—*Trans.*

DAY FOR NIGHT

"Is cinema superior to life?"

FERRAND . . . I'd like you to tell him that the auto accident we're shooting tomorrow will be done *en nuit américaine*.

JULIE What does that mean—*nuit américaine?*

FERRAND It's when you shoot a night scene, but in broad daylight. You know, by putting a filter in front of the lens.

JULIE Oh, "day for night." It's called "day for night" in English.

FERRAND Is that so? Oh, good!

A film co-produced by	LES FILMS DU CARROSSE (Paris) P.E.C.F. (Paris) P.I.C. (Rome)
Directed by	FRANÇOIS TRUFFAUT
Original Screenplay by	FRANÇOIS TRUFFAUT JEAN-LOUIS RICHARD SUZANNE SCHIFFMAN
Director of Photography	PIERRE-WILLIAM GLENN
Camera Operator	WALTER BAL
Assistant Cameramen	DOMINIQUE CHAPUIS JEAN-FRANÇOIS GONDRE
Assistant Directors	SUZANNE SCHIFFMAN JEAN-FRANÇOIS STEVENIN
Script Girl	CHRISTINE PELLE
Film Editors	YANN DEDET MARTINE BARRAQUÉ
Art Director	DAMIEN LANFRANCHI
Set Photographer	PIERRE ZUCCA
Sound	RENÉ LEVERT
Assistant Soundman	HARRIK MAURY
Dubbing Mixer	ANTOINE BONFANTI
Production Administrator	CHRISTIAN LENTRETIEN
Music	GEORGES DELERUE
Executive Producer	MARCEL BERBERT
Production Manager	CLAUDE MILLER
An Italian-French Co-Production distributed by	WARNER BROTHERS A WARNER COMMUNICATIONS COMPANY

Running Time　1 hour 55 minutes
Process　Eastmancolor,
Spherical Panavision®

Day for Night was filmed at the Victorine Studios in Nice and on location in the Côte d'Azur from late September through December 1972.

Day for Night was first shown out of competition at the Cannes Film Festival on May 14, 1973. It was also shown at the New York Film Festival on September 28, 1973. It opened commercially in Paris on May 24, 1973.

Day for Night won the 1973 Academy Award for "Best Foreign Film."

Day for Night also won the following three awards given by the National Society of Film Critics and the New York Critics' Circle:
　"Best Picture, 1973."
　"Best Director: François Truffaut."
　"Best Supporting Actress: Valentina Cortese."

Cast

The Actors Who Play Actors

JULIE BAKER-PAMELA Jacqueline Bisset
SÉVERINE Valentina Cortese
STACEY Alexandra Stewart
ALEXANDRE Jean-Pierre Aumont
ALPHONSE Jean-Pierre Léaud

The Actors Who Play Technicians

FERRAND, *the film director* François Truffaut
BERTRAND, *the producer* Jean Champion
JOELLE, *the script girl* Nathalie Baye
LILIANE, *apprentice script girl* Dani
BERNARD, *the prop man* Bernard Menez
ODILE, *the make-up girl* Nike Arrighi
GASTON LAJOIE, *the production manager* Gaston Joly

The Others

The Television Announcer Maurice Séveno
DOCTOR NELSON (JULIE's *husband*) David Markham
MADAME LAJOIE, *The wife of the production
manager* Zénaïde Rossi
The little boy with the cane Christophe Vesque
The English insurance broker Henry Graham
The French insurance broker Marcel Berbert

*Certain members of the crew also appear in the film playing
themselves.*

Description of the Characters

Julie Baker (Jacqueline Bisset)

JULIE is not present at the start of the film, but she is talked about a great deal. This young Englishwoman, who often visited France as an adolescent, is now a famous Hollywood film star, like her mother before her. (We assume that her mother is of French origin, married an Englishman, and that she retired from films a long time ago.) When JULIE arrives from America, she impresses the crew as being very sensual in appearance, yet extremely reserved in manner. For that reason alone everyone seems a bit frightened of her. Yet, for all that, JULIE BAKER is not a difficult or temperamental actress; if anything, she is rather fragile, due to the obvious nervousness she feels in unfamiliar surroundings. *Meet Pamela* marks her return to the screen after an absence of two years following a nervous breakdown. The one question in every crew member's mind: "Will Julie Baker be able to stick it out to the end?"

Séverine (Valentina Cortese)

SÉVERINE represents a breed that is fast dying: "The Star" (one could go even further and say "The Diva"). She is hyperfeminine, by turns coquettish, witty, outrageous, amusing, overemotional. Undisciplined and rather irresponsible, SÉVERINE nevertheless is greatly admired by her peers because of the fertility of her imagination and her baroque talents for improvisation. SÉVERINE always has a bottle of champagne within easy reach. But even her alcoholism is due to a terrible secret, something unbearable in her private life which all her marvelous gifts as an actress are not sufficient to make her ever forget.

ALEXANDRE (Jean-Pierre Aumont)

ALEXANDRE is French, yet the most essential part of his career took place in Hollywood, where he played romantic leads. At that time he got the nickname of "The Continental Lover" which has dogged him ever since. In those long dead days, ALEXANDRE played opposite JULIE BAKER's mother as well as with SÉVERINE. From his guarded remarks it is quite obvious that he also knew both women on a more personal level as well. Long-suffering and a truly decent man, ALEXANDRE now observes life more than he participates in it. He remains always a bit aloof, although never less than gracious, with regard to others. He finds no interest whatsoever in petty details and never talks about himself. Instead, ALEXANDRE prefers to stick to the generalities concerning his craft which in their own way politely serve to keep others at a distance. One feels that ALEXANDRE has seen everything when it comes to moviemaking, has taken part in film productions of all kinds, and that little can upset him. His secret? Well, every day, he drives to the Nice Airport, waiting for someone who seems continually to put off arriving.

ALPHONSE (Jean-Pierre Léaud)

ALPHONSE is a young French actor who recently took a course in mime in order to perfect his technique. A cinema buff above all else, ALPHONSE is usually quite excited by his work. Unfortunately, the shooting of *Meet Pamela* comes at a terrible time in his life, for ALPHONSE has been floundering about in a love affair with an independent young woman, LILIANE, whom he has gotten a job as a script girl trainee on *Meet Pamela* just to make sure she will always be around. In the same manner as children of divorced parents who go through agonies never being able to determine which was right, their father or their mother, ALPHONSE never stops asking himself: "Is love more important than work? Is life more important than films?"

LILIANE (Dani)

As well as being ALPHONSE's "little friend," LILIANE is also the youngest member of the crew. Originally attracted by the glamour of the movie world, she is now discovering its difficulties, especially the problems facing any "outsider" who lives with an actor. Gifted with strapping good health and sound common sense, LILIANE nevertheless hesitates a bit whenever she has to make an important decision. She enjoys simple relationships with the rest of the crew, and wishes them to respond to her in kind, devoid of any intrigues or complications. Her main complaint against ALPHONSE: "Just because he's had an unhappy childhood doesn't give him the right to make everybody else suffer!"

BERTRAND (Jean Champion)

Bertrand does not smoke five-dollar cigars, nor does he peremptorily summon some budding Stendhal to his office to bawl him out or tell him how to write a movie script. He is neither vulgar nor brutal, and not at all money-mad. If BERTRAND speaks respectfully of "the Americans" who are financing *Meet Pamela*, he would nevertheless not dream of giving himself airs of being "A Big Producer." Above all else, BERTRAND is conciliatory—rather sentimental, in fact. And if he has worries of his own, he hides them in order not to upset those around him. He is paternal in nature rather than paternalistic, running with a gentle hand this mad holiday camp that constitutes any French film being shot outside Paris. Yet, for all his overt calm, BERTRAND will not get a decent night's sleep until the last day's shooting is over.

FERRAND (François Truffaut)

FERRAND did his military service in the artillery; and during
maneuvers lost the use of one ear, his left, the right having been
impaired since childhood. Yet some malicious tongues say that
although FERRAND is deaf to the most loudly shouted criticism he
can always hear the most softly voiced bit of praise. FERRAND
always thinks before he speaks, but that does not mean he always
says everything he thinks. In his favor, it must be said that
FERRAND never acts high-handedly, and seems not to care in the
slightest about giving the impression of being the "Big Chief."
Shooting a film always makes him happy. It reminds him of the
only good times in his youth, those few weeks spent each summer
at a holiday camp. All the incidents that disrupt the normal day-
to-day shooting seem to stimulate FERRAND rather than annoy
him—probably because he likes to find himself cornered, backed
up against the wall, so to speak, and thus forced to improvise.
To FERRAND improvisation can only deepen the resonances of a
movie script. During the entire shooting period, his universe is
divided into two distinct groups: a) those who are good for the
film; and b) those who are not good for the film. If necessary,
FERRAND can be quite ruthless when dealing with the latter.

JOELLE (Nathalie Baye)

This young woman would not surrender her job of script girl
even at gunpoint. She lives for the film. JOELLE receives the con-
fidences of nearly every other crew member; and what she doesn't
know, she can easily surmise. She arranges all the necessary little
things the director has no time for, she pulls all the strings.
Sometimes, JOELLE even takes on the thankless role of "bitch-on-
wheels" during the shooting in order for her boss FERRAND to
continue to remain popular with the crew. FERRAND's closest col-

laborator, she identifies her needs completely with his own, protecting him from disruptive influences at the same time as she gives over her whole life to the film in progress. JOELLE is never anybody's fool, but takes no part in the rather hothouse atmosphere that builds up during a long shooting. JOELLE's complete lucidity could be very irritating were it not complemented by her great discretion. Her idea of love can be summed up in a single sentence: "I'd leave a guy for a film, but I'd never leave a film for a guy!"

BERNARD (Bernard Menez)

BERNARD is the modern equivalent of Molière's Sganarelle in our adventure: a commonsensical, vulgar, at times selfish buffoon. BERNARD is cunning and a great complainer; yet, for all that, he is extremely involved in his work, and a fine craftsman. Highly sarcastic in his dealings with the other crew members and not at all impressed by actors, BERNARD grows even more biting when dealing with women, although he remains highly attracted to them sexually. In on everything that occurs during the shooting, he is a strong and independent character, rather like some taxicab drivers. Marcel Pagnol created BERNARD's type indelibly when he set down the following credo of the prop man, as delivered by Fernandel in *Le Schpountz*: "Nobody admires the prop man enough. . . . I'm doing the only work that could ever interest me because it's a job for a madman. . . . When I look at a movie I never see the actors, I only see the props. . . . A badly chosen teapot can completely fuck up a tender love scene."

Screenplay

Translator's Note: *The original script of* Day for Night *has few technical notations. Therefore, we have thought it appropriate at times to signal differences between the final cut of the film and the script, as well as to add other notations where they seemed appropriate. When such additional information is given, however, it will always be enclosed within brackets, to indicate that it was not part of the original French-language script.*

[*The sound of an orchestra tuning up.*

The credit titles, in bright blue lettering, appear against a black background.

At the extreme left of the frame, throughout all the credits, we see two parallel vertical white lines of fluctuating width: the sound track of the film.

As the credits continue, we can hear a rehearsal of the recording of the background music score, with composer-conductor Georges Delerue stopping the musicians at times to call out cues, to give tempi, etc. The music itself is a kind of résumé of all film music, moving in less than three minutes' time from a grandiose Bach-like theme to a humorous bal musette *accordion.*

Once the credits end, a sepia-tinted still of the Gish sisters in D. W. Griffith's Orphans of the Storm (1922) *covers the entire screen. We hear the voice of François Truffaut: "This film is dedicated to Lillian and Dorothy Gish."*]

A MAIN SQUARE IN PARIS. EXTERIOR. BRIGHT SUNSHINE.

Steps leading underground to a métro station; various shops, a large colorful café, sidewalks; stone stairs leading up between two buildings to another street (not visible) upon a higher level, these stairs divided in the middle by a handrail, which makes one think the square is located somewhere on the hills of Montmartre. Much traffic. Many pedestrians.

A young man (Jean-Pierre Léaud) comes up out of the métro entrance. With a very determined stride he crosses the square. Arriving from the opposite direction, down the stone stairs, a man in his early fifties (Jean-Pierre Aumont) appears. In a few seconds both men are face to face. They stop, look at each other fixedly without speaking. The young man suddenly hits the older man hard across the face.

VOICE (*off-camera*) Cut!

As the camera pulls back we see that this has not been a scene in real life at all; but, rather, in the shooting of a movie. [As the camera tracks even further back, we see the technical crew standing around another camera: the one which has been filming the movie within our movie.] Above the façades and flimsy fronts of the various buildings we can make out the tops of palm trees. This immense Parisian square is a movie set constructed out in the open air on the lot of a Riviera film studio.

Jean-François, the first assistant director,[1] summons the extras who cluster at one end of the square to listen to criticism of the scene just shot.

JEAN-FRANÇOIS Please, everybody, gather around me! We'll have to shoot it again. I don't know what got into all of you, but this take was even worse than the one before! Everybody came

---

1. This role is played by Jean-François Stevenin, who is actually second assistant director on *Day for Night*.

Day for Night. A Parisian square, as constructed on the lot of the Victorine Studios in Nice.

dashing out of the subway in one big bunch. And you, the bus driver, you started off too late . . .

In another part of the square, even as we continue to hear JEAN-FRANÇOIS, *we see* FERRAND, *the film's director* (François Truffaut), *watching the two actors rehearse the slap: they are* ALPHONSE, *the younger man, and* ALEXANDRE, *the older.*

Not far from the café terrace we see JOELLE, *the script girl* (Nathalie Baye).[1] *Notebook in hand,* JOELLE *moves among the extras, checking things, accompanied by* BERNARD, *the prop man* (Bernard Menez). ODILE, *the make-up girl* (Nike Arrighi), *stands alongside* ALEXANDRE, *sticking on his false mustache, which has become unglued during all the slaps he has received from* ALPHONSE.

Later, we see JOELLE *explaining her duties to* LILIANE, *the apprentice script girl* (Dani), *as they both pore over a big notebook.*

JOELLE   It's very simple. You mark the footage at the beginning of each shot, then the footage at the end. Also, the length of each take. You circle the ones the director decides to print.

LILIANE   Who do I give all this info to?

JOELLE   No one. You keep it as your own record.

While WALTER, *the director of photography,[2] has some of the lights on the set changed,* PIERROT, *the set photographer,[3] walks over to take some photographs of* ALPHONSE *slapping* ALEXANDRE.

[*Camera zooms to a TV antenna high above the back of the set. The camera then cuts to a group of men standing behind one of the flats.*] *We see now that a television crew has also been setting up its equipment.*

[1. The script girl is responsible for recording the details of each take in order to insure that no discrepancies occur in the continuity when the film is edited. In the U.S. this job is usually called "continuity girl (or man)."]

2. Role played by Walter Bal, who is actually the camera operator on *Day for Night.*

3. Role played by Pierre Zucca, who holds the same job in the crew of *Day for Night.*

Shooting *Meet Pamela*. In the foreground, left to right: JOELLE, the script
girl (Nathalie Baye); the assistant director (Jean-François Stevenin); and
the director (François Truffaut).

Directing the actors.

The television announcer (Maurice Séveno) *is improvising a "lead-in" before his own TV camera.*

ANNOUNCER Good morning, ladies and gentlemen. I'm standing here on the lot of the Victorine Studios in Nice, where I'm about to watch the first day's shooting of the film *Meet Pamela*. Unfortunately, for us the title is a misnomer, for we won't be meeting Pamela today, since the young artist, Julie Baker, who plays this important role, is still in Hollywood. Nevertheless, all the other leading players are here, and I hope to be interviewing them shortly.

At that very moment, BERTRAND, *the producer* (Jean Champion), *arrives, with* ALEXANDRE *in tow.* ALEXANDRE *is still rubbing his cheek.*

ALEXANDRE (*joking*) Oh, no, its's nothing serious. I'll only have a swollen cheek for the next three weeks, that's all!

The two men laugh. BERTRAND *introduces* ALEXANDRE *to the television announcer, then quickly moves out of camera range.*

ANNOUNCER Sir, since you're the producer of this film, please remain. I'd like to interview you, too. Come on. Tell us all about *Meet Pamela!*

BERTRAND (*still trying to get away*) No. No. A producer should always remain in the background.

The announcer, finally giving up, turns to ALEXANDRE.

ANNOUNCER Would *you* care to tell us what *Meet Pamela* is about?

ALEXANDRE Well, it's the story of a man in his early fifties who has a son. This son has recently married a young English girl and is now bringing her home to meet his parents.

ALEXANDRE'S *face, in close-up, is suddenly replaced on the screen by that of* ALPHONSE, [*standing in exactly the same position, looking in the same direction, although with a different background behind him*].

ALPHONSE Well, it's the story of a young man who marries an English girl. Three months after his marriage, he decides to introduce her to his parents, who are staying at their seaside villa.

ALPHONSE'S *face is replaced by that of* ALEXANDRE.

ALEXANDRE The character I play falls madly in love with his daughter-in-law, and she in turn with him.

Back to ALPHONSE'S *face.*

ALPHONSE . . . and there, the young girl falls in love with her father-in-law . . .

Cut back to ALEXANDRE'S *face.*

ALEXANDRE . . . and the film depicts the affair of the adulterous couple.

Cut back to ALPHONSE'S *face.*

ANNOUNCER (*off-camera*) Yes? And then? What happens then?

ALPHONSE Well, I believe the story is treated in a tragic manner. And therefore, as in all tragedies, each character must work out his own destiny to the end.

Cut back to ALEXANDRE'S *face.*

ALEXANDRE I'm sorry to cut this short, but I believe I'm needed on the set.

We are back on the huge Parisian square.

FERRAND *has walked over to the camera.*

FERRAND All right, places, everybody! We're shooting. Roll 'em!

JOELLE *runs out before the camera and holds up the clapboard.* [*The clapboard is a hinged board on which are recorded the scene and take numbers. At the start of each take it is held up before the camera and clapped to make a starting point in the sound track. This point is then synchronized with the image of the closed board.*]

JOELLE *Pamela,* one, take two.

We see another take of the scene with which the film opened. Only this time the action is commented upon by the director through a megaphone.

FERRAND (*off-camera*) Send in the bus. . . . Newspaper vendor, look more alive! . . . Lady with the little dog, a bit faster. . . . Go ahead, Alphonse! . . . Red auto, quick, get out of the shot! . . . Careful, Walter, be ready to zoom in on Alexandre!

The take continues up to the slap.

Now a series of close-ups of the slap with only ALPHONSE *and*

ALEXANDRE *involved. At the seventh take of the slap* FERRAND *seems satisfied. He announces to the extras that the crowd scene is to be done once more, only this time as a crane shot.*

The camera is set up on a traveling crane by the grips. The scene can thus be photographed from a high angle, with the camera moving up, down, and even laterally. The crane is an enormous red apparatus which blocks part of the street.

After some brief commands, "Quiet . . . camera . . . action!" JOELLE *rushes out with the clapboard. The extras begin to move around the square once more.*

The camera moves slowly upward on the red crane [the movement paralleled, of course, by the camera photographing this camera photographing the scene!] and in the background we no longer hear any of the everyday sounds connected with shooting but, instead, a sprightly Vivaldi-like music [that also "lifts" as the crane moves higher and higher].

Hotel Atlantic. Interior. Night.

This hotel, situated in the heart of Nice, is where most of the actors and technical crew of Meet Pamela *are quartered.*

[In the background can be heard the sound of a switchboard operator: "Hotel Atlantic . . . just one moment, I'll connect you. . . ." Indeed, these sounds from the switchboard will be heard from now on, as a kind of aural punctuation, during all of the scenes taking place in the Hotel Atlantic. They subtly serve to remind the viewer that he is no longer at the Victorine Studios, and that, difficult as it may be to believe, there are other things in the world besides moviemaking.]

In the hotel lobby, bending over the main desk, ODILE *is attaching some stamps to postcards.* JOELLE *arrives and begins questioning the young desk clerk.*

JOELLE I have a room with a bath and I'd prefer one with a

shower. Would it be possible for me to exchange with some-body else?

But before the desk clerk can answer:

ODILE   I have a shower in mine but I'd much rather have a tub.

JOELLE   Perfect! We'll arrange it between ourselves then, huh?

ODILE   Sure.

JOELLE   Good! Come on, we can go up together right now!

The two young women head for the stairs. They disappear from view even as they continue discussing the relative merits of their rooms.

On another floor we see FERRAND *turn a corner. He suddenly stops short before a blue vase containing a bouquet of dried flowers which serves as decor in the long corridor. Before he can make a decision he is joined by* ODILE, *[coming up from the floor below]. She hands him a packet of photographs.*

ODILE   Joelle gave me these just now.

FERRAND   Ah, yes, the photos of Julie! Thank you, Odile, thank you very much!

ODILE *disappears.* FERRAND *calls over* WALTER, *who has just come strolling along the corridor. During this first evening it seems as if the entire crew is at loose ends, wandering about, trying to meet up with each other.*

FERRAND   Oh, Walter. Here are the photos of Julie I asked for. Come and have a look.

They examine them together: various publicity stills of JULIE BAKER, *the young actress who will play the title role in their film and whom none of them has yet seen.*

WALTER   But I know her already. I saw her in that film—you know, the one with the wild car chase?[1] Wasn't she very sick not so long ago?

[1. This is just one example of the film's Pirandellian quality. Jacqueline Bisset, who plays JULIE-PAMELA, was the feminine lead in Peter Yates' 1968 film, *Bullitt,* which features a spectacular car chase. One wonders, also, if Truffaut did not choose the name "Julie" as a kind of homage to another English actress, Julie Christie, with whom he

FERRAND Yes. She had a nervous breakdown of sorts. But that's already a year and a half ago.

WALTER All the same, I remember hearing she walked out on the film she was making right in the middle of shooting!

FERRAND Yes, she did. But since then she has married her doctor. So I'd imagine things have gotten much better for her. There's every reason to hope so, anyway.

WALTER And Bertrand isn't worried?

FERRAND No, I don't think so. He trusts me. (*glancing over the stills*) Here, look at this one. Isn't she lovely?

WALTER Aren't there any of her wearing a short wig? I'd like to see how she photographs that way.

FERRAND That's right, she'll be playing Pamela in a wig.

WALTER She has such fine eyes, don't you think? They catch the light. . . .

FERRAND Yes. Clear eyes . . . green, very green. It's unbelievable how much she resembles her mother!

WALTER Oh, I remember her, too. She was very beautiful. Such good bone structure . . . perfect for the camera.

FERRAND But Julie's equally beautiful. In fact, perhaps a bit more so. Because not only does she have that same sad, haunting quality, but she can also project at the same time a definite . . . sexiness. And that's most important of all for an actress, don't you think?

Their conversation is suddenly interrupted by BERNARD. *He is holding in his hand a candle upon which he has made some improvements.*

BERNARD Monsieur Ferrand, I'd like to show you my trick candle.

FERRAND Oh, yes . . . for the fancy-dress sequence. O.K. Show us how it works, Bernard.

BERNARD *turns off the lamp in the corridor. Then he takes the cord attached to his candle and plugs it into the wall socket. He hands the candle to* WALTER, *who lights the wick with his*

---

had such splendid relations on the set of *Fahrenheit 451*. For that matter, the leading characters in *The Bride Wore Black* and *Mississippi Mermaid* are also named Julie.]

Jacqueline Bisset (JULIE-PAMELA).

cigarette lighter. The trick is a very clever one: the body of the candle has been hollowed out, concealing a tiny lamp of high wattage that can be hidden from the camera even while it illumines the face of the character holding the candle. Although his demonstration is convincing, BERNARD's *words are rather confused, his thoughts running ahead of his speech.*

BERNARD There, you see! The actress has to hold the lamp directly toward her face so you think it's the candle that's lighting her up. But she's got to be very careful the light is opposite the camera, or otherwise, you see, and then this cord has to be hidden in her dress up her sleeve, while she faces—

FERRAND (*good-naturedly cutting him short*) Agreed, Bernard! O.K. You've sold me on the idea!

BERNARD *"disconnects" his candle and relights the corridor lamp. Just as he is about to dash off,* FERRAND *stops him.*

FERRAND One second, Bernard. What do you think of this vase?

FERRAND *takes out the bouquet of dried flowers and hands the blue vase to* BERNARD.

FERRAND It's not bad, is it? You know, I've been thinking how much I'd like to see that vase in Séverine's dining room in the film!

BERNARD (*examining it*) But it's cracked.

FERRAND All the more reason for taking it! And, remember, not one word about it to anybody![1]

BERNARD *goes off with the blue vase.* WALTER *follows, in order to get further lighting particulars concerning the trick candle.*

At that very moment ALPHONSE *and* LILIANE *are on their way to their room, chatting happily.*

FERRAND *profits from their passing to conceal the last trace of his theft: he holds out to* LILIANE *the bouquet of dried flowers.*

FERRAND Here, Liliane. I've a present for you!

LILIANE Why, thanks! . . . I'd also like to thank you for letting me work as an apprentice script girl on your film.

FERRAND Does the idea of being a script girl please you?

[1. The subtitler of the U.S. version added a rather witty flourish here. In the subtitles FERRAND says: "Let's take evasive action!"]

LILIANE Well, uh, you know, after just one day of shooting I can't tell yet.

FERRAND I've found that it's a wonderful job. You'll see!

LILIANE I'll let you know two months from now!

FERRAND Yes. Well, see you later, kids.

LILIANE *watches* FERRAND *disappear down the corridor, then she pulls* ALPHONSE *closer.*

LILIANE You never told me your director was deaf!

And, indeed, FERRAND *does wear a hearing aid in his left ear.*

ALPHONSE What do you mean, deaf? He got an ear loused up when he was serving his time in the artillery, that's all!

LILIANE Oh.

ALPHONSE *kisses* LILIANE *lightly, then whispers into her ear.*

ALPHONSE Come on, Liliane, do me a favor, huh? Walk on a little ahead of me—so I can watch your ass! Go on!

LILIANE How? Like this?

She walks down the corridor, rolling her hips, undulating her buttocks humorously. An old woman resident of the hotel passes by with an astonished look. As for ALPHONSE, *he's in seventh heaven.*

ALPHONSE Yes, yes! Just like that. Oh, that's good! That's *very* good!

They enter their room. At the same time a young chambermaid is leaving. ALPHONSE *lingers in the doorway to watch the chambermaid walk down the hall.*

When he finally joins LILIANE *in the room, she lays into him, half teasingly—but only half.*

LILIANE I caught you!

ALPHONSE Caught me what?

LILIANE Feeling up that little maid in your mind! So that's the type you go for, huh? The kind that waddles like a little rubber duck? You bastard!

ALPHONSE Little rubber duck? Come on, you're not going to be jealous, are you?

LILIANE Not at all. I'm never jealous. In fact, I find jealousy is something for idiots! Either that, or else you have to carry it all the way to its logical end—murder. No. If anyone's jealous, it's you!

ALPHONSE Me?

LILIANE Yes, you! It's quite obvious. Your eyebrows meet in the center of your forehead.

As she speaks, ALPHONSE *has gone into the bathroom. He examines his face in the mirror.*

ALPHONSE My eyebrows do *not* meet in the center of my forehead!

He comes out again. LILIANE *has thrown the dried flowers onto one of the beds and has already sat down upon the other.*

ALPHONSE Don't you think these twin beds look sad separated? Wouldn't they be happier side by side?

LILIANE (*looking around her*) Wait. Before doing that we've got to move this table first.

And so ALPHONSE *and* LILIANE *set to work.*

LILIANE You know, you could have asked them for a room with one big bed! I told you to.

ALPHONSE Yes, but to do that I'd have had to go to Lajoie, the production manager.

By this time the first brass bed has been moved. They now attack the other.

ALPHONSE Never accuse me of being an actor who isn't "moving"![1]

The two beds are finally side by side. By this time every other piece of furniture has been disarranged. ALPHONSE *sits down, puffing.*

ALPHONSE Whew! . . . What are we doing for kicks tonight?

LILIANE Oh, I thought we might go to one of those picturesque little eating places up in the hills above Nice. You know, the kind where they grill things over an open fire, with fennel and

---

[1. The French pun here is unfortunately lost in the translation. ALPHONSE describes himself as an actor "qui déménage"—a verb in French which not only means "to move furniture around" but also "to go batshit, off one's rocker."]

tarragon and everything. Pierrot, the photographer, gave me a list of some out-of-the-way restaurants he says are really first-rate. . . .

ALPHONSE　What's all this? I don't think I'm hearing correctly!

LILIANE　Well, we've got to eat somewhere, haven't we?

ALPHONSE *has stood up and now he begins pacing back and forth across the room.*

ALPHONSE　You know, sometimes you're really beyond me! Here we have the good luck to be staying in a city where there are thirty-seven movie houses—thirty-seven! And yet you want to spend all our free time eating! My idea was to choose a film from the newspaper listings, run over to the theater right now to find out when it goes on again, and then, if we've got any time left, to grab a sandwich at the nearest corner bar. As for your photographer with his list of picturesque little restaurants in the hinterlands where they grill everything over wood fires, you can tell him to stuff it up his—

LILIANE　No, it's not possible! You know something? You kill me! You really do! In any case, I'm warning you right now. I am *not* going to any movie tonight, and I am *not* going to eat here in the hotel, either! So, I leave it up to you. It's *your* move!

LILIANE'S *decisive air has succeeded in calming* ALPHONSE. *He goes up to her, repentant.*

ALPHONSE　All right. I give in. We'll do what you want. But only on one condition.

LILIANE.　I'm still listening. What's that?

ALPHONSE *walks over to where the bouquet is lying on the bed. He pretends to pick something from the bouquet and then ceremoniously returns with this invisible "flower" to present it to* LILIANE.

ALPHONSE　That you marry me.

The screen fades to black.

This is the end of the first day's shooting of Meet Pamela. *And also, for that matter, the end of the first day's action of* Day for Night.

VICTORINE STUDIOS. EXTERIOR. MORNING.

FERRAND *has asked* ODILE, *the make-up girl, to play a small role in* Meet Pamela. JEAN-FRANÇOIS, *the first assistant director, is having her model the costume she is to wear. As* ODILE *holds it up [over the smock she continually wears throughout the film,] the two men talk.*

JEAN-FRANÇOIS Not bad. What do you think?

FERRAND Not bad at all. I'm sold. I'll buy it.

ODILE *herself seems quite satisfied with her maid's costume: short black dress, white lace apron, white lace cap. She takes a few tentative steps holding it around her, swaying prettily.*

On the huge standing set of the Parisian square FERRAND *can now be seen emerging from behind a section of a flat. He comes toward the camera, thinking to himself.*

FERRAND (*voice-over*) Shooting a film is exactly like crossing the Old West in a stagecoach. At first you hope to have a good trip. But, very soon, you start wondering if you'll even reach your destination.

FERRAND *is interrupted in his musings by a short man* (Gaston Joly) *who comes bustling up to him.*

LAJOIE Ah, good morning, monsieur! Excuse me for bothering you but . . . I think perhaps you don't recognize me, monsieur? I'm Lajoie, your new production manager.

FERRAND Oh, yes. Yes, of course.

LAJOIE What I'm concerned about right now is the automobile to be used in the accident sequence. You'll have to choose one of these two.

LAJOIE *leads* FERRAND *over to two convertibles: one a bright red, the other an immaculate white.*

FERRAND The white one would do perfectly—if we could only have it painted blue. Is that possible?

LAJOIE It's possible—for two hundred thousand francs.[1]

FERRAND That much just to paint it blue? No. We'll keep it as it is. (*he takes a few steps around the car*) Still, it seems awfully white all the same.

FERRAND *suddenly notices a blue convertible parked a short distance away.*

FERRAND Ah, why didn't you show me this one?

LAJOIE Oh, no! Impossible! That one belongs to your assistant director, Jean-François!

FERRAND Jean-François, eh? Well, he might just agree to it. Would you ask him?

FERRAND *leaves* LAJOIE *standing there, confused, and continues his walk.*

FERRAND (*voice-over*) What is a film director? A film director is someone who is continually being asked questions—questions about everything. Sometimes he has the answers. But not always.

This time it is the art director[2] of Meet Pamela *who interrupts* FERRAND *in his reflections.*

ART DIRECTOR Were you satisfied with the way I fixed up the square?

FERRAND Yes, it was fine. You were absolutely right, Damien. Then, too, we had such wonderful luck with the weather. So it worked out even better. Everything went off perfectly.

ART DIRECTOR I know, I was watching. I'd like to show you the bungalow. . . .

[1. Although the franc was devalued in 1959 to one hundredth of its former amount, many Frenchmen still persist in using old francs in conversation. Here, two hundred thousand *ancien francs* is equal to two thousand *nouveau francs*—or, at the fluctuating exchange rate of the dollar in 1972 when the film was made, approximately $450.]

2. Played by Damien Lanfranchi, the actual art director on *Day for Night*.

FERRAND (*quickening his steps*) All right, let's get it over with right now.

ART DIRECTOR (*stopping him*) Oh, no! The set itself hasn't been constructed yet! I meant the sketches.

FERRAND Oh, the sketches . . .

The art director opens a satchel filled with designs which he has been carrying under one arm. The two men stand motionless as they look over the designs for the bungalow.

ART DIRECTOR The interior will be completely workable: that is, there'll be a bed, two night tables, some chairs, a cutaway ceiling. . . .

FERRAND Wait. I'm sorry, but I've got to stop you. I can guarantee the camera will never once go inside the bungalow. We're shooting the entire scene through the window. Therefore, all that we'll ever truly see is the bed. That's all that counts: the bed.

[*In that way, of course, a great deal of money can be saved. And the camera, by remaining at a discreet distance from the illicit lovers, can give the scene added power. Just one example of* FERRAND's *genius for improvisation when faced with a tight budget.*]

The art decorator goes off, satisfied; and now it is BERTRAND, *the producer, who latches on to* FERRAND.

BERTRAND Ah, here you are, Ferrand! I don't want to bother your head with all this, but—I've just talked again with the Americans. They insist we stick to the original schedule. The film has to be shot in seven weeks. Do you think you can do it?

FERRAND It's not going to be easy. Seven weeks!

BERTRAND Well, of course, if you need three or four days' extra for matching shots using a reduced crew, I suppose it won't be the end of the world. But we must definitely have our actors free on October 31st.

FERRAND October 31st? Listen, I'd better check the shooting schedule again with Jean-François. But O.K. Agreed. Seven weeks!

FERRAND *and* BERTRAND *separate.*

FERRAND (*voice-over*) Seven weeks . . . five days a week, thirty-five days. I'll never be able to shoot a film as complicated as this one in thirty-five days!

Now it's ODILE's *turn to break in upon* FERRAND's *reflections. She holds up a wig before his face.*

ODILE I'd like your opinion. This is Séverine's wig. Don't you think the color's too light?

FERRAND Frankly, I couldn't say. You might see Joelle, and Joelle can ask Walter. He's the one who'll be photographing it. The two of them should be able to come up with some solution. Right?

ODILE Yes. Right!

Hardly has FERRAND *gotten rid of* ODILE *than he is set upon by* JEAN-FRANÇOIS, *all out of breath.*

JEAN-FRANÇOIS The prop man wants to show you another one of his gismos.

Even as he speaks, JEAN-FRANÇOIS *has been leading* FERRAND *over toward* BERNARD, *who stands holding a tray upon which a number of weapons are deployed.*[1]

BERNARD Here—I've picked out five. . . . You know, for the revolver to be used at the end.

FERRAND Oh yes, the revolver at the end.

BERNARD Well, which one?

FERRAND Let me see. It's for Alphonse. He doesn't have very large hands. But, no. I won't take the smallest. How about the next to the smallest—that one there?

And FERRAND *hands the prop man the revolver that will "play" an important role in the film's final scene.*

A short while later, we see the Parisian square [in a long shot] completely empty, [palm trees behind the false fronts fluttering in the wind]. We can hear the rasping of a loudspeaker echoing over the lifeless set: "The crew of Meet Pamela *is to report to the screening room immediately."*

[1. Behind the three men in this shot in the actual film can be seen a street sign: PLACE DE CHAILLOT. This is a nod on Truffaut's part, one assumes, to the fact that the immense outdoor set was originally constructed in 1969 for Bryan Forbes' *The Madwoman of Chaillot*.]

SCREENING ROOM. INTERIOR. DAY.

The "rushes"[1] are shown in a tiny auditorium on the lot. When we arrive, most of the crew of Meet Pamela *is already seated. The first assistant director,* JEAN-FRANÇOIS, *finally closes the door, after having stood outside in the corridor checking who is still missing. Entering with him are* WALTER, *the director of photography, and* JOELLE. JOELLE *carries with her the precious satchel which never leaves her side and in which she keeps all data pertinent to the film.*

FERRAND *enters and goes to sit next to the film editor.[2]*

FERRAND Greetings, Yann! What are we going to see today?

YANN The scene between Séverine and Alphonse: "I'm going to kill them both."

FERRAND And how about the crowd scene on the square—"the slap"?

YANN No, sorry. It hasn't come back yet. We only received two reels.

FERRAND That's odd. (*turning around in his seat*) Tell me, Bertrand, why haven't we received any film using the big outdoor set—you know, the scene of "the slap"?

BERTRAND (*to the production manager*) Lajoie, get Paris on the phone. Ask the lab what's holding them up.

JOELLE This is sequence number ten.

While awaiting LAJOIE's *return,* FERRAND *decides to view the*

[1. "Rushes" are the results of the previous day's shooting, first prints made from sound and picture negatives separately for checking action, photographic quality, and camera technique.]

2. Played by Yann Dedet, one of the two film editors on *Day for Night*.

*rushes which have arrived. He casts a final glance around to
see if anyone is still missing.*

FERRAND   Where's Séverine?

ODILE   Oh, Séverine never watches her rushes!

FERRAND   Oh, I see. Fine. (*calls out*) Roll 'em!

The lights go out.

FERRAND (*leaning toward* JOELLE)   I see we don't have Alexandre,
either!

JOELLE   He's probably at the airport. As usual.

FERRAND   What's he always doing at the airport?

JOELLE   Search me. He goes there every day—obviously to wait
for someone. If you ask me, he's got some problems in his
private life.

*The screening of the rushes begins. On the screen [the image
surrounded on all four sides by black, to indicate that what
we're seeing is on a movie screen] there appears, first of all,
a clapboard, held up by a grip.*

GRIP   "Pamela, ten, one, second take."

We now see ALPHONSE *slowly coming down a flight of stairs inside a house. He walks over to a divan upon which* SÉVERINE *sits.*

[*The print we are viewing is still quite rough, with the color
not yet "balanced." The lighting appears rather harsh and flat,
making both* SÉVERINE *and* ALPHONSE *look cadaverous.*]

ALPHONSE   "Mama, I must talk to you. I must talk to you about
them. Does that bother you?"

SÉVERINE   "Yes."

ALPHONSE   "All the same I have to talk to you. I know where they
are now. I've found them. They're in Paris. What's more,
they're not even trying to hide."

SÉVERINE   "Why are you so stubborn, my little one? Do as I do:
cast them out of your thoughts."

ALPHONSE   "I can't. I can't think of anything else any more."

SÉVERINE   "How would you like it if we went on a trip? Just the
two of us—far, far away? You know I would do whatever you
wish."

Valentina Cortese (SÉVERINE) and Jean-Pierre Léaud (ALPHONSE).

ALPHONSE "No. My decision is made, Mama. I'm going up to Paris. And I'm going to kill them both."

In the darkness ALPHONSE *watches his image up on the screen with great concentration. He mouths each line with the character.* [*He does not seem very pleased with his performance.*]

The rushes continue: another take of the same sequence.

YANN (*leaning over toward* FERRAND): I think that for the line "they're not even trying to hide" this take is better.

While the screening goes on, LILIANE *reaches over and takes* PIERROT's *cigarette from his hand.* (*The set photographer is sitting at her right while* ALPHONSE *is on her left.*) *Even though* ALPHONSE *is still very involved with his character up on the screen, he hardly appreciates this sign of intimacy between* LILIANE *and* PIERROT. *He places a tender, yet "proprietorial" hand inside* LILIANE's *thigh. As the rushes of this take end and the lights come on again,* LAJOIE (*who has just returned*) *whispers something in* BERTRAND's *ear.*

BERTRAND (*standing up*) Kids, we've a big technical foul-up. There was a power failure while developing the film at the Paris lab. The crowd sequence in the square was completely ruined. It has to be reshot from beginning to end.

The crew gets out of their seats with various exclamations of disappointment and disgust. They leave the screening room. Only FERRAND, JOELLE, *and* JEAN-FRANÇOIS *remain, gathered around* BERTRAND.

BERTRAND The question now is: When can you shoot it again?

JOELLE The only time available would be the day after tomorrow.

JEAN-FRANÇOIS What? We can't start reshooting before Monday! I need time to dig up 150 extras in Nice! It's not possible before then!

FERRAND (*to* BERTRAND) Will the insurance cover us?

BERTRAND I hope so! You know, my friend, if you want to make any money these days you have to be in real estate, not movies! If I continue in this racket much longer, it'll only be because I find it very invigorating!

The door of the screening room closes upon BERTRAND.

VICTORINE STUDIOS. PROFESSIONAL BUILDING. INTERIOR. DAY.

We see ALEXANDRE *climbing the stairs leading to the corridor along which are the doors to various actors' dressing rooms. As he arrives at the first landing, he runs into* BERTRAND *who is carrying a small portable television set.*

ALEXANDRE Good morning! That's a nice little thingamajig you've got there. Is it for me?

BERTRAND (*laughing*) No, sorry! Not for you!

Just then LAJOIE *arrives, out of breath as usual, a huge bouquet in his hand. The flowers are magnificent, but they have been wrapped in an old newspaper.*

LAJOIE The bouquet you wanted for Madame Séverine, sir.

BERTRAND What's wrong with you, man? You think I'd bring them in to her in that shitty wrapping? Go and make me a real bouquet!

The production manager leaves, very confused, while BERTRAND *and* ALEXANDRE *resume walking up the stairs.*

ALEXANDRE Er, tell me something—I assume Séverine knows that I'm to play opposite her?

BERTRAND Of course. She was delighted.

ALEXANDRE Ah, good. . . . So much the better.

BERTRAND But why don't you go in right now and say hello to her yourself?

ALEXANDRE There's nothing I'd like better. Which one is her dressing room?

BERTRAND *leads him to a door* [*upon which there is a white card with blue lettering:* SÉVERINE].

ALEXANDRE *hesitates a moment as* BERTRAND *disappears down the corridor. He nervously arranges his neck scarf, then knocks.*

Within, SÉVERINE *is putting on her make-up, with* ODILE's *help. She turns to face the door.*

SÉVERINE (*singing out*) En-trez!

ALEXANDRE *enters, smiling.* [*He clicks his heels humorously and makes a little bow.*] SÉVERINE *gets up from her chair and with one wild bound hurls herself into his arms.*

ALEXANDRE Séverine!

SÉVERINE Alexandre! (*in English*) My darling, my love! (*reverting to French*) Oh, how happy I am to see you!

ALEXANDRE *and* SÉVERINE *stare at each other for a long moment, in absolute silence. Then* SÉVERINE *throws back her head and begins to laugh. In order to hide her confusion, she begins to speak in a veritable spate of words, haphazardly mixing French, Italian, and English.*

SÉVERINE *E tu, vecchia puttana!* [And you, you old whore!] . . . what have you been doing in order to *conservati cosi bene* [keep yourself looking so trim], eh? . . . Listen, darling, I'm so glad to be working with you again!

ALEXANDRE And I also, with you! Do you remember—that first time we met in Hollywood?

SÉVERINE *Tais-toi!* (*in English*) Shut up! (*reverting to French*) When you're around me, never, repeat *never*, utter a single date, mention a single year—or I'll go around telling everybody you've had your face lifted!

ALEXANDRE (*laughing*) Not yet—but perhaps very soon!

SÉVERINE You know that for you—only for you!—I would be capable of cooking again! *Ti ricordi il mio risotto alla milanese?* [Do you remember my risotto alla milanese?] You loved it so much once!

ALEXANDRE (*with a straight face*) Ah, well, as a matter of fact, I no longer do.

SÉVERINE (*truly anxious*) *Cosa?* [What?]

ALEXANDRE No, I'm only kidding! I will be very happy to eat your risotto alla milanese!

Talking all the while, SÉVERINE *has accompanied* ALEXANDRE *to the dressing room door.*

SÉVERINE Will we two be working together today?

ALEXANDRE No. Not today. Today you'll be working with Alphonse. As for myself, I'm off to the airport. We'll see each other tomorrow.

They embrace warmly.

Having shut the door behind ALEXANDRE, SÉVERINE *returns and sits down before her make-up table, alongside which* ODILE *has been standing all the while. [Among the many photographs propped up against the mirror we can make out, in a place of prominence, one of* SÉVERINE *sitting beside a young boy (her son). It is only later on in the film that this photo, never seen again, will assume a particular poignancy.]*

SÉVERINE Isn't Alexandre adorable! I acted with him, oh, twenty years ago, back in Hollywood. We were both there during the same era. You must have heard, haven't you, that Alexandre was a great charmer, a regular seducer!

ODILE Really?

SÉVERINE Oh, yes! (*laughs*) In Hollywood in those days they called him "The Continental Lover"! Oh, I loved him a great deal myself then!

ODILE Is he married?

SÉVERINE Funny. I don't know. He *was* married—twice. And twice divorced. Perhaps he's living with someone now, but nobody knows much about his private life. He's so secretive!

ODILE He has to wear a mustache in the film. As for me, I like him better with the false mustache. What do you think?

SÉVERINE Oh, mustache or no mustache, he still plays romantic roles. . . .

SÉVERINE *examines her face in the mirror without the slightest trace of vanity.*

SÉVERINE And look at me! Now I'm stuck with this old mug . . . the "abandoned woman" kind of face, desperate, tragic—a real pain in the ass!

ODILE But you're so beautiful!

SÉVERINE Oh, my God, what a horror I am! Help me, my child, help me rehearse today's scene! I can no longer remember any of the words!

And, as if to give herself courage, SÉVERINE *refills her glass of champagne that is on the make-up table beside her.*

SÉVERINE I don't know why—but my memory seems to be so fucked up lately!

We now return to the corridor outside the dressing rooms. On a partly open door we can read: JULIE BAKER.

BERTRAND *and* FERRAND *enter this dressing room.* BERTRAND *puts the portable television set on the make-up table.* FERRAND *looks around, examining the room [which is much grander than* SÉVERINE*'s. On the wall to the left of the door as they enter is a huge black-and-white blow-up of Léon Gaumont (1863–1946), founder of Gaumont Productions and responsible for the construction of the first film studio in Nice in 1914].*

FERRAND This dressing room is truly lovely. It's magnificent, in fact. Large, spacious . . . yes, a very handsome room, Bertrand! Only some flowers are missing.

BERTRAND Don't worry, I've already taken care of that, too! You know, I admire this Julie Baker as much as you. You wanted her for the film, so I got her for you. But if she doesn't finish our film, we'll be up shit creek without a paddle!

FERRAND *(as if not hearing)* What's that?

BERTRAND She underwent a physical examination and the doctor of the insurance company refused to insure her. He found her to be still too nervous and asked that we postpone shooting for another month.

FERRAND What did the Americans tell you?

BERTRAND Oh, luckily, the Americans are easier to deal with than the French in these matters! They agreed to run the risk with us. But if she cracks up, I'm warning you they won't take the blame—it's us who'll be standing in the front row when the shit hits the fan!

FERRAND Yes—I agree. But, when you come right down to it, if we didn't believe in luck, we'd all of us be working in some other business, wouldn't we?

Valentina Cortese and Jean-Pierre Aumont (ALEXANDRE).

BERTRAND All the same, we're taking a big risk. . . . Oh, by the way, have you spoken about the rushes with Séverine?

FERRAND Yes. I dropped by her dressing room earlier to say hello.

BERTRAND You knew, I suppose, that Alexandre and she once had a big thing going between them?

FERRAND Yes. I think I heard something about it.

BERTRAND It was notorious. A wild affair. The papers never stopped writing about it. And then, as you might expect, it ended badly. For four years no producer could ever get them to work in a film together, they hated each other so much. But, a lot's happened since then. . . .

As they have been chatting, BERTRAND *and* FERRAND *have come back to the open door of* JULIE BAKER's *dressing room.* AL-PHONSE *is now standing just outside.*

ALPHONSE (*to* FERRAND) Do you have five minutes?

FERRAND Yes. Of course.

ALPHONSE (*to* BERTRAND) You haven't forgotten my check, have you?

This must be a standing joke between them, for the producer laughs: "I haven't thought of anything else for days!" as he departs. ALPHONSE *has led* FERRAND *back into* JULIE's *dressing room in order not to be overheard.*

ALPHONSE I'd like to ask you something. (*looking around*) Oh, this is some swell dressing room! A hell of a lot better than mine!

FERRAND (*smiling*) Yes. It's Julie's.

ALPHONSE (*suddenly serious*) You know, Liliane and me—we're going to get married.

FERRAND Oh? Good—very good! That makes me very happy.

ALPHONSE Yes. I finally decided. We're going to be married here, in Nice, before the end of shooting. That's the reason I wanted to see you. Er—it wouldn't irritate you to be our best man?

FERRAND Not at all. Quite the contrary. It would make me very happy.

ALPHONSE Then it would make me very happy, too.

BERNARD *suddenly enters. He has come to show* FERRAND *the blue vase earlier "pinched" from the hotel, which he has patched up beautifully.*

BERNARD Before I put this on the set I want your opinion. What do you think?

The camera moves in on the vase. It fills the screen.

SET: "SÉVERINE'S DINING ROOM."

At first all we see is the blue vase as it is being set down upon a low table by BERNARD. *Then* BERNARD *lights the fire in the fireplace. The logs are real, even if they conceal a gas pipe linked by a hose to a bottle of butane behind a screen. All* BERNARD *has to do to obtain the illusion of a fire that has been carefully tended for hours is to turn on the gas tap and then toss a lighted match into the fireplace.*

SÉVERINE, *a glass of champagne in one hand, watches* BERNARD *regulate the height of the flames.*

SÉVERINE I can't take my eyes away from that fire!

FERRAND You know, I think people once stared at fires the way they do at television sets now. What's more, I've a feeling that men and women have always needed, especially in the evening after a meal, to look at flickering images.

SÉVERINE It's true! I never thought of that. . . .

While preparations for the shot continue (we can see WALTER *arranging the lighting with the gaffer),* FERRAND *happens to run into* LILIANE.

FERRAND Oh, Liliane, Alphonse has already told me. I'm very pleased. I congratulate you—all my best wishes!

To judge by the shocked look on LILIANE's *face, as soon as* FERRAND *has moved on, she has no idea what he is talking about.*

While waiting for shooting to begin, FERRAND *asks* BERNARD *to turn off the fire, as it has been smoking up the set. The logs*

On the set of *Day for Night* during the shooting of the sequence in
SÉVERINE's dining room. In the foreground, left to right: François Truffaut,
Jean-Pierre Aumont, Nathalie Baye, Valentina Cortese.

have caught fire by this time; and so now we have the rather surprising sight of BERNARD'*s hands moving down from inside the top of the fireplace, dousing the flames with a spray can.*

At the other side of the set we find FERRAND, *whose path is now blocked by an officious little man* [*in a spruce blue suit, matching trilby, and outrageous boutonnière*] *brandishing an immense script. The man is accompanied by two young women who sport the same long hair* [*one bleached blonde, the other dyed red*], *the same vacuous smiles, and the same loud make-up that gives them the appearance of two identical dime-store dolls.*

OFFICIOUS LITTLE MAN Good day, Monsieur Ferrand! I would like you to meet two charming young ladies. They're from Germany, and are sisters: Greta and Diana. This one here has just finished a very important political film in Germany. Why don't *you* make political films?

FERRAND Er, well . . .

OFFICIOUS LITTLE MAN And this one has made an erotic film, a great success also. Why don't *you* make an erotic film? I also have here with me a fascinating script dealing with pollution. . . .

JEAN-FRANÇOIS *suddenly comes over and places himself between* FERRAND *and the little man.*

JEAN-FRANÇOIS If you'll excuse me, sir? Ferrand, will you please come over here, something isn't working right.

He leads FERRAND *away.*

FERRAND Why, what's wrong?

JEAN-FRANÇOIS Nothing. Nothing at all. But I thought you might need being "liberated"!

Now it is BERTRAND *who intercepts* FERRAND.

BERTRAND Oh, Ferrand. I'd like you to meet Monsieur Giacometti.

He introduces Ferrand to a man seated next to him who seems to be watching with great curiosity everything that is happening on the set.

BERTRAND Monsieur Giacometti, Monsieur Ferrand.

FERRAND How do you do, monsieur. Delighted.

BERTRAND Would you have a minute to spare, Ferrand?

FERRAND No, sorry, not right now. This shot is tricky. Afterwards, perhaps?

FERRAND *leaves the two men and rejoins* JEAN-FRANÇOIS.

FERRAND Who in the hell is that character Bertrand's brought along with him?

JEAN-FRANÇOIS A big-wheel member of the fuzz. It's thanks to him we've got an authorization to shoot in the streets of Nice. That's why Bertrand's brought him over. Makes the man feel important with his cronies, you know, spending a day watching us shoot.

FERRAND That may be a lot of fun for him watching us shoot—but do I go and watch *him* shoot? Do I go and watch while he "interrogates" some prisoners?

FERRAND *mimics in a quite unmistakable manner (shaking a clenched fist against an invisible jaw) a "serious" police interrogation, causing* JEAN-FRANÇOIS *to burst out laughing.*

Finally, everything is ready for the "serious rehearsal" of the sequence to be filmed. Walter announces, "Ready to roll anytime!" FERRAND *approaches* SÉVERINE *in order to inform her personally.*

FERRAND (*quietly*) As soon as you're ready, Séverine.

SÉVERINE (*in English*) Yes. O.K.

And she takes her place on the set—but not before emptying her champagne glass.

FERRAND Quiet on the set, everyone! This is a serious rehearsal.

JEAN-FRANÇOIS Quiet!

The set represents an elegant dining room. ALEXANDRE *is seated at the table with a cup of coffee. Some dishes have already been cleared, as the scene takes place at the end of a meal. [There remain a coffee pot, a bottle of wine, and a colorful bowl of fruit in the center of the table.]*

ALEXANDRE *smokes a cigarette, combating his wife's mounting hysteria (the wife played by* SÉVERINE, *of course) with an imperturbable, stolid silence.*

The camera is set up on a dolly on the outer edge of the set.

SÉVERINE *stands on her "mark," beside a chair, her back to the camera.*

FERRAND (*whispering*) Go ahead, Séverine!

SÉVERINE "Frankly, I don't understand you, Alexandre. You've been . . ." (*she hesitates*)

ALEXANDRE (*quietly prompting*) "Odd."

SÉVERINE (*in English*) Oh, shit! . . . Odd.

FERRAND Nothing serious. Let's start over.

SÉVERINE *once again takes her place standing by the chair.*

SÉVERINE "Frankly, I don't understand you, Alexandre. You've been odd for a long time now. Last night, when you walked out in the middle of dinner, that was very rude to Julie." (*in English*) Oh, shit! I said Julie instead of Pamela![1]

While she has been delivering her speech, SÉVERINE *has moved about the room, until now she has reached the fireplace, before which she stops, realizing her error.*

FERRAND Nothing too serious.

SÉVERINE No, it's not working at all for me. Listen, Ferrand, I've a better idea. Why don't I act it out, but recite numbers instead? I always do it that way when I work with Federico![2] Listen . . .

And before FERRAND *can stop her,* SÉVERINE *has taken her place on her "mark" once more. She now gives a brilliant demonstration, roaming all over the set, sweeping her arms about grandly, moving with great authority . . . but replacing all her lines with numbers: "Seven, twelve, thirty-seven, etc." She stops only after reaching the fireplace, where she ended her speech before.*

SÉVERINE (*turning to* FERRAND) It works fine that way, doesn't it?

FERRAND (*going over to her*) No, Séverine, it's not possible.

[1. One can sympathize with Séverine's confusion here. For if Julie Baker plays a character named Pamela, the actor Alexandre is playing a character named . . . Alexandre.]

[2. Valentina Cortese did play, in her own professional life, Giuletta Masina's mystical friend Valentina in Federico Fellini's *Juliet of the Spirits* (1965).]

SÉVERINE   But why not?

FERRAND   It's fine, but we can't. No.

SÉVERINE   Oh, you're completely lacking in a sense of humor! You can always post-synch my lines later, and then I'll recite your lovely dialogue, comma for comma!

FERRAND *can not stop himself from laughing, charmed by the woman despite himself. Still, he remains adamant. With one hand he brings down the boom upon which the microphone is attached.*

FERRAND   We don't do it like that here in France. You have to speak your lines. See? . . . we record direct. No. We must find another solution.

SÉVERINE   Listen, it's *your* fault . . . because you always give me my lines at the very last minute! Wait! I've an idea. Why not cue cards?

FERRAND   We can try it that way.

SÉVERINE *calls over* JOELLE *and dictates her speech to the script girl.* JOELLE *stands by the table on the set and hurriedly scribbles the text in large letters on various sheets of paper. Not far away,* BERNARD *cuts cigarettes in half with a pair of scissors. [These cigarette halves are to be used by* ALEXANDRE, *a new one at the start of each take, since he is to smoke continually throughout the scene.]*

JOELLE (*quietly, to* BERNARD)   Cut up a lot. I've a hunch we're going to need all of them!

BERNARD   What do you think I *am* doing?

JOELLE *walks around the set, attaching the cue cards to various walls, according to* SÉVERINE'*s directions. The other crew members look on rather cynically.*

JOELLE   Here, Séverine, how's this? Can you read it here?

SÉVERINE   Yes, that's fine.

JOELLE   Good. And then, this last one, remember, will be behind that column.

Once more they are ready. FERRAND *has by this time decided to shoot the scene without any further rehearsal.* JOELLE *comes and stands before the camera, holding up the clapboard.*

Valentina Cortese, Jean-Pierre Aumont, and Nike Arrighi (ODILE).
"I no longer know if Odile is my make-up girl or if she's an actress . . ."

FERRAND (*quietly*)   Go ahead, Séverine. Any time.

SÉVERINE   "Frankly, I don't understand you, Alexandre. You've been odd for a long time now. Last night, when you walked out in the middle of dinner, that was very rude to . . . Pamela. No matter how you feel about her, she *is* Alphonse's wife. One might think you hated her, the way you purposely avoid talking to her!"

Except for her hesitation over the name "Pamela," SÉVERINE *has played the scene with remarkable ease, moving from one concealed cue card to the next without ever being obvious. The crew holds its breath. . . .*

This is the moment in the scene when ODILE, *dressed as the maid, enters on cue to clear the table.* SÉVERINE *rushes toward her.*

SÉVERINE   "What do you mean, coming in here like that? Can't you see I'm talking to Monsieur? Get out!"

ODILE *rushes from the room.*

SÉVERINE (*turning to face Alexandre*)   "And that's something I will not stand!"

SÉVERINE *is about to leave the dining room, making a grand exit, slamming the door behind her. But, suddenly, she becomes confused and flings open the door of the china cupboard instead.*

FERRAND   Cut!

SÉVERINE (*still not realizing her error*)   Oh, I got through it! It went well, don't you think?

FERRAND   No. Not exactly. I mean, Séverine, it went very well— but, you see, that's not the right door.

SÉVERINE   Oh, I thought it was the same one!

FERRAND *calmly explains her error to* SÉVERINE. *Shooting begins all over again* [*with* ALEXANDRE *using a new cigarette half after discarding the one still in his mouth*].

The second take goes wonderfully well. But, at the end, SÉVERINE *opens the cupboard door once more.*

This time ALEXANDRE *gets up and goes over to* SÉVERINE *and quietly shows her the correct door.*

ALEXANDRE Listen, my darling, look at them carefully. I know the two doors look rather alike, but—

SÉVERINE *Lo so* [I know] . . . It's not that one, it's *this* one! (*in English*) I understand—I'm not an idiot, after all!

ALEXANDRE *resumes his place at the table.* SÉVERINE *remains standing beside the two doors. She suddenly reaches out and embraces* BERNARD *tightly.* (*The prop man had earlier come over to dull with a spray a section of the door which was picking up too much light for the camera.*)

SÉVERINE Oh, Bernard, you're the only person here who understands me! You can come and see me later in my dressing room. . . .

She kisses him. BERNARD *finally succeeds in prying himself loose. As he hastens away, he makes a gesture to the crew with his right hand twisting his nose, indicating that* SÉVERINE *is completely sozzled.*

The third take. SÉVERINE, *despite her condition, plays the scene remarkably—but again makes the same mistake over the two doors at the end.*[1]

FERRAND (*to* JOELLE) It's all messed up. She'll never get it right.

By now SÉVERINE *has grown irritable. She directs her wrath upon the first person available: little* ODILE.

SÉVERINE I tell you it's not my fault, Ferrand! I no longer know if Odile is my make-up girl or if she's an actress. That's enough to upset anyone! In my day make-up girls remained make-up girls, and actresses were actresses! That's what has been mixing me up!

[*Little* ODILE *puts her hand to her mouth, not knowing what to do or say.*]

FERRAND It's going to be all right, Séverine. We'll just take a breather for a few minutes.

[1. In watching the scene in the film itself, one can not but wonder why FERRAND did not cut away from SÉVERINE before her last line, to a reaction shot of ALEXANDRE, then film her grand exit separately later on. Admittedly, some of the power of the tirade is dissipated if it is broken up that way—but it would have saved the poor woman's being so cruelly humiliated before the entire crew.]

SÉVERINE No, it's *not* going to be all right!

FERRAND *directs* JEAN-FRANÇOIS *to clear the set of all visitors. The assistant director does this more bluntly than* FERRAND *might have wished.*

JEAN-FRANÇOIS (*loudly*) O.K., everybody not having a reason to be here—out! Scram!

And, what's more, he begins pushing people toward the exit. [We see the two German girls, Greta and Diana, rushing off, along with their "protector."]

FERRAND *has noticed* ALPHONSE *leaving. He goes over to him and explains that he is certainly welcome to remain. But* ALPHONSE *prefers to leave, too. It gives him a good excuse to return to Nice to see a movie.*

LILIANE, *who has been entering information concerning the various takes in her notebook, leans over toward* JOELLE, *as they both sit alongside the camera.*

LILIANE If you ask me, it's her own fault. She doesn't have to hit the bottle like that!

JOELLE Put yourself in her place. Her son is dying of leukemia. Every day she's scared she'll be getting a telephone call. . . . She hesitated a long time, for that matter, before signing for this film—because of that.

Once more the shooting commences. The crew no longer feel like joking. The atmosphere is thick enough to cut with a knife.

In the middle of the take, SÉVERINE *breaks down, sobbing hysterically.* FERRAND *calls out, "Cut!" and goes over to comfort her.*

FERRAND No, Séverine, it's going to work out fine. You'll see. We'll just stop now for a little while.

SÉVERINE (*sobbing*) I don't know what's happening to me. Maybe it's this wig. It's giving me a terrible headache!

She tears off her wig. Her own hair is held tightly against her skull by a net. The face SÉVERINE *now lays bare to the camera is that of a tragic Pierrot.*

ALEXANDRE *comes over and takes* SÉVERINE *in his arms, whispering softly, trying to calm her.*

SÉVERINE (Valentina Cortese): the face of a tragic Pierrot.

FERRAND, *visibly discouraged, decides to let the crew off for the rest of the day. They'll attack the scene in earnest tomorrow morning.*

[ALEXANDRE *and* SÉVERINE *are standing to the far left of the now empty set. The camera lens begins to close at the far right of the frame, serving as a kind of mask (or wipe), moving toward the left until three-quarters of the screen is black, with only* ALEXANDRE *and* SÉVERINE *visible, in the dim light, at far left.*]

[*The lens closes completely. Fade out to black.*]

HOTEL ATLANTIC. INTERIOR. NIGHT.

We are in a dark bedroom. It's obviously the middle of the night. FERRAND, *trying to sleep, continues to hear voices which seem to be pursuing him.*

VOICE OF BERTRAND (*off-camera*) I spoke with the Americans. We absolutely have to finish the film in seven weeks as originally planned. . . .

VOICE OF OFFICIOUS LITTLE MAN (*off-camera*) Why don't you make a political film? Why don't you make an erotic film?

Suddenly, in FERRAND's *dream, a little boy* (Christophe Vesque) *appears. He walks alone down a deserted street in the middle of the night. He is carrying a cane much too big for him.*

[*The cane makes a tap-tap-tapping sound as the little boy walks. The shot of the little boy is in black and white, although printed on color stock.*]

[*Before the boy reaches his destination (if he has one), the screen suddenly comes alive in bright color: the main gate of the Victorine Studios, early morning.*]

VICTORINE STUDIO. EXTERIOR. DAYLIGHT.

*On the studio lot a swimming pool has been fitted out to serve
as a set for Meet Pamela. Surrounded by hastily planted shrubs
and flowers, it now represents the garden behind the villa of
ALPHONSE's parents.*

*FERRAND is walking along the edge of the pool, checking out
the look of the set. He notices a dour-looking woman (Zénaïde
Rossi) seated on a folding chair. She knits furiously even as she
talks to LAJOIE, the production manager. FERRAND decides to
question JEAN-FRANÇOIS.*

FERRAND Tell me, Jean-François, who's that woman I keep seeing
everywhere?

JEAN-FRANÇOIS It's the production manager's wife. She follows
him everywhere, she never gives him a minute's peace. This
isn't the first film I've come across her. If you like, I can try
and get rid of her.

FERRAND No. No. I'm beginning to get used to her.

*FERRAND and JEAN-FRANÇOIS disappear out of camera range,
just as JOELLE arrives with STACEY (Alexandra Stewart), the
young actress who will be playing ALEXANDRE's private secretary
in Meet Pamela. STACEY doesn't seem in a happy mood, and
JOELLE is trying to calm her.*

STACEY To tell you the truth, I don't know why Ferrand chose
me for this film. He hates me! He's never been able to stand
me! And then—

JOELLE Where did you ever get such a silly idea?

STACEY I'm sure of it. What's more, he thinks I'm a lousy actress.
(*laughs*) Just between you and me, he may be right about that!

JOELLE No, listen . . .

STACEY I'm sure it wasn't Ferrand who chose me. It must have been the producer. When I come right down to it, I don't understand anything that's been going on here! There's something very bizarre about this film!

JOELLE I never heard Ferrand mention anyone except you for the part.

STACEY (*somewhat mollified*) Really? You're certain of that?

JOELLE I assure you. . . . Now, come on.

Calm now, STACEY *walks back with* JOELLE *toward the shooting area. But, before she does, she throws a quizzical glance at* ALPHONSE *and* LILIANE *who are having a heated discussion [standing beside a small inboard motorboat that looks oddly unsettling as it rests upon a trailer in this unused area of the lot].* ALPHONSE *and* LILIANE *are too preoccupied to notice that anyone can overhear them.*

ALPHONSE The things you've been pulling lately have completely destroyed my morale! I can't take all this shit, I tell you!

FERRAND *has come over to greet* STACEY, *and to discuss the forthcoming scene. It seems nothing is working out here, either.*

STACEY I'm sorry. I'm very sorry. But I was hired to play a secretary, not a bathing beauty! There was never any mention of my having to wander around half-undressed—never! If you want proof of that, I didn't even bring a bathing suit along when I packed! If you want my frank opinion, a secretary who goes around taking baths in her boss's pool is—well, ridiculous! No, I assure you, it's not possible. I won't do it!

FERRAND Listen, Stacey, perhaps it wasn't written that way in the original script—but in my opinion the scene plays better that way. Alexandre has invited his secretary to his villa during her vacation. It's all quite logical. She's being treated as a guest, not as an employee. At the opening of the scene, you are in the pool, enjoying yourself. Then Alexandre has an urgent letter to send off, and so he calls you over to dictate it to you. What's so odd about that?

STACEY I'm sorry, but it's not possible. It's not a question of my being . . . stubborn or willful. I was asked to learn how to type for this role and, you know, I even took lessons! But there was never any talk of pool dips or swimming! I won't go into the water and I won't wear a bathing suit—and that's the end of it!

FERRAND *abruptly leaves* STACEY *and her imprecations and goes over to* JOELLE.

FERRAND   Joelle, find me another scene to shoot right now. Let's give that idiot time to cool off.

JOELLE   There's no other scene we can shoot until Julie Baker arrives. We have to film the swimming pool sequence today.

FERRAND   All right. Agreed. Would you go over to her then and try to convince her? And, what's more, explain to her that in 1972 an actress who refuses to appear in a bathing suit is, well, grotesque!

A little while later we have the surprise of discovering STACEY *cavorting in the water.* JOELLE *obviously succeeded in her mission. The sequence seems to proceed without a hitch:* SÉVERINE *reads her telegram, informing her husband of the news [that* ALPHONSE *is bringing his English bride for a visit], and* ALEX-ANDRE *calls* STACEY *out of the pool to dictate his letter [to the real-estate agent, asking to rent the villa next door for the newlyweds].*

The camera tracks back on rails which extend over the pool. FERRAND *and* JOELLE *follow the scene with great attention. Suddenly* JOELLE's *look becomes even more penetrating. She grabs* FERRAND.

JOELLE   I see now why she didn't want to put on a bathing suit! Look at her!

FERRAND   She's very lovely.

JOELLE   You haven't understood anything. Look at her more closely!

FERRAND   Good God!

Studio production office. Interior. Day.

FERRAND *and* BERTRAND *are in the middle of a stormy session.*

FERRAND That Stacey hoodwinked us all! She's three months' pregnant, and she deliberately didn't tell anyone! I want her contract canceled and another actress hired right now!

BERTRAND I don't agree! Frankly, I don't think it's all that obvious she's pregnant.

FERRAND Wait a minute, Bertrand. Come over here and take a look at our shooting schedule. (*He leads the producer to a huge chart upon the wall.*) Stacey still has one day more to work with us, then she leaves for five weeks. By the time she comes back, she'll be five months' pregnant—and it'll be obvious to the camera! No, it's not possible, we must get another actress. You know yourself it's not all that difficult. We can select one right now and then call her agent. Here are loads of lovely young women . . . more lovely young women. . . .

As he speaks, Ferrand is flipping through the pages of a Film Casting Directory.

BERTRAND Listen to me. Stacey has an airtight contract. I'd like nothing better than to phone her agent, but I already know I'd be the one who finally ended up eating crow! And do you want to know why? Because life, unhappily, is made up of enforced relationships. Might makes right!

LAJOIE *enters, setting down a package before* FERRAND.

FERRAND Oh, these are the books I asked for!

[FERRAND *has already forgotten his anger in his childish delight over the package.*] *A telephone rings.* LAJOIE *answers it, then holds out the receiver to* FERRAND.

LAJOIE It's the composer calling from Paris. Will you take it?

FERRAND Of course. Hello, Georges, is that you?[1]

VOICE (*off-camera*) Hello! I'd like you to listen to a playback of the music for the fancy-dress sequence.

FERRAND *holds out the supplementary earpiece of the telephone to* BERTRAND *while he himself continues to listen through the receiver, [which he holds not up to his ear but down alongside the amplifier of his hearing aid, which is attached to his rolled-up left shirt sleeve].*

FERRAND (*to* BERTRAND) The playback. You know, for the fancy-dress sequence.

Even as he listens, FERRAND *has been spreading out upon the desk the contents of the package: books (mostly in French but a few in English) devoted to the work of various film directors —Carl Dreyer, Ernst Lubitsch, Ingmar Bergman, Jean-Luc Godard, Alfred Hitchcock, Roberto Rossellini, Howard Hawks, Robert Bresson, [Luis Buñuel, Luchino Visconti[2]].*

The music ends.

FERRAND Fine, Georges! I'm truly very pleased! Thank you very much. Until later then!

FERRAND *hangs up.* BERTRAND *has donned his jacket and is preparing to leave the office.*

FERRAND What do you think? It sounded fine, don't you agree? I'm very happy with Georges' music.

BERTRAND Yes, fine. But the airport . . . Julie's plane . . . the press conference . . . I mustn't be late.

[1. Georges Delerue, who actually composed the music for *Day for Night,* also wrote the scores for *Shoot the Piano Player, Jules and Jim, Love at Twenty, Soft Skin, Two English Girls,* and *Such a Gorgeous Kid Like Me.* One of France's most talented and prolific composers, Delerue also wrote such other important film scores as those for Godard's *Contempt,* Malle's *Viva Maria,* and De Broca's *King of Hearts.*]

[2. "For me the essential people are Renoir, Rossellini, Hitchcock . . . although they don't seem to have much in common. I also admire Howard Hawks, Ingmar Bergman, Luis Buñuel, Orson Welles, Robert Bresson—each for his own quality, his own particular strong point." ("An Interview with François Truffaut." *Cinéma 64,* no. 89, September-October 1964.) Truffaut's 1969 film, *Mississippi Mermaid,* was dedicated to Jean Renoir.]

BERTRAND *is already almost out of the door. A sudden thought stops him.*

BERTRAND Tell me something. You're famous for improvising in your films. Why couldn't Alexandre's secretary be pregnant in the movie?

FERRAND Yes. That might work. No, wait a minute. Impossible. The audience would immediately think Alexandre was the father. Or, worse yet, that her pregnancy had some bearing on the plot. No, it's impossible!

BERTRAND Stacey isn't married, is she? Then I wonder who *is* the father of her child . . . ?

On this unanswered question BERTRAND *slams the door behind him.*

[*The camera quickly pans across the room. As it does so, there is a sudden staccato flickering of light and the beginning of a low rumbling music.*]

[*Abrupt cut to a stock shot of a plane landing in bright sunshine. The flickering continues even as the music grows more pounding.*]

NICE AIRPORT LOBBY. INTERIOR. DAY.

Many flashbulbs popping. [*We suddenly realize that they have caused the flickers of light in the previous shots. The music in the background is exciting, if ominous, like the sound of summer thunder upon the horizon or the swarming of bees.*]

The jostling and pushing of reporters and photographers is reminiscent of Hollywood premières during the motion picture capital's heyday.[1]

[1. It will surely take nothing away from Truffaut's own brilliant handling of the scene to mention that it echoes George Cukor's opening sequence (the Hollywood benefit) in *A Star Is Born* (1954) and

JULIE BAKER *has just got off her plane. She is being attacked from all sides. [Some of this is shown in first-person hand-held camera shots, as seen from* JULIE BAKER'*s point of view.]*

BERTRAND *is in the front rank, of course, holding an enormous bouquet of red roses. He is having a great deal of trouble trying to protect his young star. [*JULIE *does indeed look rather frail, and this pandemonium would be enough to unhinge even the strongest nature.]*

BERTRAND *leads* JULIE *to one of the airport's lounges.*

We are now in a tiny room, filled to bursting with reporters and photographers. They are not only seated on folding chairs but they also dangle from window sills, and many others stand leaning against the walls.

JULIE *is sitting behind a long table, flanked on either side by* BERTRAND *and the publicity man for* Meet Pamela. *Ten or so microphones stretch out before her.*

PUBLICITY MAN You can ask Mademoiselle Baker your questions now, gentlemen.

JOURNALIST Would you tell us a little about the film you've come to make here in Nice?

JULIE *Meet Pamela* is the story of a young Englishwoman who falls in love with the father of her husband and who runs away with him. I'm not certain, but I believe the scenario was suggested by an actual news item.

REPORTER (*with a slight English accent, although in French*) And how does this scenario end?

JULIE Since it's a tragic story it ends unhappily. But I would prefer not to reveal any of the details.

Although JULIE *has a slight English accent, she expresses herself quite well in French.*

ANOTHER REPORTER Mademoiselle Baker, do you honestly think today's public will be interested in a film about a young woman

Lana Turner's triumphant entrance after a film première in Vincente Minelli's *The Bad and the Beautiful* (1953), in which a similar popping flashbulb effect was used.]

who has nothing more important to do with her life than go to bed with her father-in-law?

The question has been rather aggressively delivered, and JULIE *appears thrown by the reporter's hostility. She hesitates a moment before answering. [She leans over and whispers something to* BERTRAND, *who counsels her.]*

JULIE Monsieur, when I like a script enough to agree to act in it, I naturally think an audience will like it also.

[WOMAN] JOURNALIST Do you really believe what you're saying?

JULIE Of course! I not only believe it, I certainly hope it's true!

ANOTHER REPORTER I hope you'll forgive me for using this occasion to pry into your private life—but, all the same, we've been reading rather disturbing reports in the American newspapers. For example, that Mademoiselle Baker, in fragile health, married her doctor.

JULIE I did not marry my doctor. I married a man who happens to be a doctor.

JOURNALIST Why isn't this lucky man here with you now?

JULIE But he is. He's here, at this very moment, in this very room.

VOICE He's here? Where?

JULIE I can't tell you. He hates publicity.

JULIE *gives a happy little laugh, more sure of herself once again. All the reporters turn around in their seats, scrutinizing each other, trying to find out which one of them might be* JULIE BAKER's *husband. [And* JULIE's *husband is indeed sitting in the second row from the front. He turns around in his seat, too, as if looking to find out which one of the men he might be!]*

PUBLICITY MAN That's enough, messieurs! On this little note of mystery, let us depart and allow Mlle. Baker to get to her hotel. Thank you all for coming!

Disappointed, the reporters and photographers begin leaving the room. The publicity man and BERTRAND *escort* JULIE *to the door.*

PUBLICITY MAN Let them all leave first. We'll go out to our car afterward.

BERTRAND   It went quite well, didn't you think?

JULIE suddenly stops a man (David Markham) *who is going out the door with the newsmen. He is in his early fifties: a handsome man, with a strong, intelligent face and a head of white hair.*

JULIE   Oh, Michael!

Taking him by the hand she leads him over to BERTRAND.

JULIE   I'd like you to meet my husband, Doctor Nelson.

She smiles.

VICTORINE STUDIO. EXTERIOR. DAY.

One of the key scenes of Meet Pamela *is being shot: the arrival of* ALPHONSE *and his young bride at his parents' villa. The camera and crew are all installed on the second story terrace of the villa set, looking down upon the lawn and driveway.*

FERRAND is just about to call out, "Roll 'em!" when he notices, sitting in the middle of the driveway below, LAJOIE *and his wife.* MADAME LAJOIE *is ensconced on her eternal folding chair and knitting her eternal sweater.*

FERRAND   If you please, madame, could you back up eight or nine feet? You're in the camera range right now. Thank you, madame!

While MADAME LAJOIE *moves further away, aided by her husband,* FERRAND *turns to* JOELLE.

FERRAND   That woman is unbelievable! She's always here!

JOELLE   Didn't anyone tell you? She's the production manager's wife.

FERRAND   Yes, yes, I know. But all the same, she's never absent. Is she studying to take over his job, or what?

JOELLE   She's insanely jealous. She thinks all of the women here are trying to make him. She poisons his whole existence. He should dump her, of course, but he hasn't the guts. You want to know what the crew call them? "The Sorrow and the Pity"!

JOELLE *and* FERRAND *laugh.*

FERRAND *suddenly notices* LILIANE *standing alongside one of the trees in the garden below. She and* PIERROT, *the photographer, are kissing.*

FERRAND What's going on over there? Now that's something I don't like the looks of at all!

Luckily, ALPHONSE *is too far away to notice. Outside the gate leading up to the villa set he and* JULIE *sit in an automobile [the blue convertible belonging to* JEAN-FRANÇOIS] *waiting for the shooting to start. They profit from this free time to get to know each other.*

ALPHONSE This is your first day. Have you *le trac?*

JULIE (*smiling*) I don't understand. What's *le trac?*

ALPHONSE (*in English*) Stage fright. Do you have stage fright?

Before we can hear JULIE's *answer, we are once again back on the villa terrace.* FERRAND *is watching, with growing irritation,* LILIANE *being pawed by the photographer.*

FERRAND (*calling out*) Enough of that, Liliane! You've got to handle the clapboard to begin the scene! We're waiting, Liliane!

WALTER That photographer's certainly not wasting any time on this picture!

LILIANE *tears herself away from* PIERROT *and runs to hold the clapboard up before the camera. Shooting begins.*

LILIANE *Pamela,* number ten, take one.

Upon a sign from JEAN-FRANÇOIS [*who has been standing just outside camera range in the driveway below*] ALPHONSE *drives the convertible through the gates in front of the villa and stops before a flight of curving stone steps leading up to the main entrance.* ALPHONSE *gets out of the car, then comes round to open the door for* JULIE-PAMELA.

SÉVERINE (*off-camera*) "Hello, there! Darling, the children have arrived!"

Jacqueline Bisset and Jean-Pierre Léaud.
"I'd like you to meet Pamela . . ."

ALPHONSE (*to* JULIE) "There are my parents."

The young couple look up.

The camera pans to the top of the curving steps where SÉVERINE
and ALEXANDRE *stand, waiting.* ALPHONSE *and* JULIE-PAMELA
walk up to meet them.

ALPHONSE "I'd like you to . . . meet Pamela."

ALEXANDRE "You are most welcome!"

SÉVERINE "Oh, my dear, I know you'll be very happy here! It's a
shame, though, the house is so small. Come out on the balcony.
Look, you can see the ocean. What do you think of our view,
my dear?"

She leads JULIE-PAMELA *out onto the terrace while* ALEXANDRE
and ALPHONSE *remain talking in low voices in the room behind
them.*

SÉVERINE "You know, my son never tells me anything. He's never
even told me how you two met!"

JULIE "Really?"

SÉVERINE "Yes!"

JULIE "Well, I was on a vacation in Yorkshire with two cousins:
Dorothy and Elisabeth. He wanted Dorothy to go out for a
drive with him—but she caught chicken pox, and so I went
in her place!"[1]

SÉVERINE "Although I don't know Dorothy, I'm still very happy
that it was she and not you who caught chicken pox!"

ALEXANDRE (*suddenly coming out onto the terrace*) "Who caught
chicken pox?"

SÉVERINE "Guess!"

[1. This speech has so many resonances. First, Jacqueline Bisset
caught chicken pox in Stanley Donen's *Two for the Road* (1967),
thus ceding her own place to Audrey Hepburn in their mutual pursuit
of Albert Finney. Then, too, the Yorkshire setting reminds one of
Truffaut's own *Two English Girls*, with its peculiar Brontëan echoes.
For that matter, the name of one of the actresses who played one-half
of the eponymous *Two English Girls*, Stacey Tendeter, probably
suggested to Truffaut the name for Alexandra Stewart's character in
this film.]

FERRAND Cut!

SÉVERINE (*dissatisfied*) Oh, shit!

FERRAND It wasn't bad, but let's try it another way.

ALEXANDRE (*to* FERRAND) I didn't come in too soon, did I?

ALPHONSE We're going to shoot it again? But why? It was good, wasn't it?

And, without waiting for FERRAND's *answer,* ALPHONSE *hurries off.*

FERRAND Let's set up the camera differently this time, Walter.

In order to leave the terrace SÉVERINE *lifts her legs carefully over the camera tracks that have been laid down all over the set.*

FERRAND (*off-camera*) You can go and take a rest, Séverine.

JULIE *remains alone for a moment, sitting on the low balustrade of the balcony.* [Camera moves in for a close-up of her pensive face.]

JULIE (*voice-over, in English*) I'm going to have to do some home-work with my French!

ALPHONSE *has rejoined* LILIANE *in the garden below.*

ALPHONSE Who was it that got you your job, huh? Why do you think I had you taken on as apprentice script girl? I wanted us always to be together, that's why!

LILIANE Oh, you and your charity! You never thought of what I might like, did you? I'm not interested in being a script girl! I'm learning nothing! What I'd really have liked was a job as an apprentice editor!

ALPHONSE You had only to tell me that! I'd have gotten you that job!

On the second floor of the villa they are setting up the camera in the middle of the room that looks out upon the terrace. FERRAND *passes the set photographer.*

FERRAND Oh, Pierre, you're finally here! You've come to take some pictures, is that right?

PIERRE Yes, sir.

From the symmetrical terrace where various technicians are

arranging the next take, we can see SÉVERINE, *settled in an armchair at the far end of the room. She is about to get up to pour herself a glass of champagne when she changes her mind.*

SÉVERINE Odile! Take away that goddamned bottle! I don't want to have to look at it any more!

ALEXANDRE *has come to sit down alongside* JULIE *on the balcony.*

ALEXANDRE And how's your dear mother these days?

JULIE Oh, fine. Just fine. I told her we'd be working together. She sends you her love.

ALEXANDRE That's kind of her. She's a marvelous woman. Everyone loved her in Hollywood. What a pity she retired from the business so soon!

JULIE All the same, she's very happy. She's occupied with a million things.

ALEXANDRE You know, she could never resign herself to this routine of working in bits and pieces. I remember escorting her to the première of her first big Hollywood film. A fantastic night! And yet, the minute after the lights came up, she stared up at the screen, then turned to me. "Did I really do all of that?" she asked. "All I can remember now is the waiting!"

JULIE Oh, yes! How true that is!

In the garden below the discussion between ALPHONSE *and* LILIANE *continues. Only now it is an outright battle.*

ALPHONSE You don't have to tell me what's going on! I'm no fool! This morning, for instance, I'm looking at you, suddenly the shot is over—and you're no longer there! I keep wondering where you've gone off to—and I've a good idea!

LILIANE Where do you want me to be?

ALPHONSE Oh, I don't know any more! I tell you, I don't know any more!

LILIANE Stop shouting!

ALPHONSE I'm *not* shouting! I'm very calm. I'm listening very calmly to whatever explanation you have to give me. (*losing his temper once more*) All the same, it would be nice if you weren't always on the make for every guy on the set!

78 . . .

FRANÇOIS TRUFFAUT

LILIANE Now that's a goddamned lie!

ALPHONSE What it comes down to is that I'm in a constant state of agony! I stand before the camera, I recite my lines like a sleepwalker, the shot's done—and all I can think of is, "Thank God *that's* over with—so now I can find out where Liliane's disappeared to!" I run everywhere, hunting for you. I don't know what I'm doing any longer, I'm in such a state!

On the terrace the cameraman is ready. But, of course, AL-PHONSE is still missing.

FERRAND (*to* JOELLE) I'm getting tired of this. Alphonse is never here when we need him!

JOELLE I think I know where he is.

And JOELLE leads FERRAND over to the balustrade and points down to where ALPHONSE and LILIANE stand in the garden, their voices louder than ever.

ALPHONSE Here's a perfect example. Right now I have to go and act. Now you tell me: what condition am I in to give a performance? I should be *cool* in this scene, and yet—

FERRAND Alphonse! We're waiting!

ALPHONSE (*to* LILIANE) If I'm terrible in this shot, you have only yourself to blame!

He leaves LILIANE. While the crew stands around, a plane takes off from the Nice Airport and passes over them with a loud roar.[1]

We are now in front of the parents' villa set. The sun is not so strong any more. The day's shooting is over.

FERRAND *and* ALEXANDRE *stroll down the curved steps conversing.*

FERRAND I'm sorry, old man, to have to make you die one more time in a film!

[1. Although the shot of the plane serves as a perfect punctuation mark with which to end the scene, it also has another meaning. The Victorine has been slated for closing in the near future. One of the reasons given (aside from the sad state of the motion-picture industry in France in general) is that it is too close to the Nice Airport, especially now that the runways are being expanded to allow for the landing of jumbo-jets.]

Jacqueline Bisset and David Markham (DOCTOR NELSON).

ALEXANDRE   Oh, I've grown quite used to it! In the eighty films
I've made, I've died eighty times: twice in the electric chair,
twice by hanging, a couple of stabbings, some suicides—and
I can't recall how many auto accidents! I've yet to die a natural
death, though. Still, I like it better this way. I don't find any
death natural.[1]

DOCTOR NELSON, *who has come to pick up* JULIE, *meets the two
men.* ALEXANDRE *leaves* FERRAND, *but not before having shaken*
NELSON's *hand warmly.*

FERRAND   Ah, good afternoon, Doctor! You're looking for Julie?
She shouldn't keep you waiting long. She's changing right now.

NELSON   Did it go well today?

FERRAND   Yes, thank you, very well. I'm very happy. You know,
until now I've never made a movie with an actress I hadn't met
beforehand. But it's working out fine. Even while appearing
quite fragile, Julie has a certain air of determination which fits
the character she's playing perfectly. I'm very pleased. Everything should work out well. See you later, Doctor!

FERRAND *hastens off.*

JULIE *comes down the front steps of the villa [she is now
wearing a blue denim outfit of matching jeans and jacket] and
joins her husband. They walk over toward their car. Suddenly,
after looking around first to make certain no one is watching,*
JULIE *leads* DOCTOR NELSON *into the shrubbery.*

NELSON (*in English*)   Is there anything wrong?

JULIE (*smiling, in English*)   I just wanted to kiss you.

And that's exactly what she does.

[1. ALEXANDRE's speech is a pastiche of one that Humphrey Bogart
was fond of reciting to reporters concerning his own screen demises.]

VICTORINE. THE CUTTING ROOM. EXTERIOR. LATE DAY.

This scene takes place immediately after the preceding one. We are near the office building within which is located the cutting room.

FERRAND, *who has just left* DOCTOR NELSON, *rushes up to* STACEY. [*She has been talking with* BERNARD, *the prop man, who hurriedly leaves upon* FERRAND'S *arrival.*]

FERRAND Oh, Stacey, I'm sorry. I've kept you waiting.

STACEY It doesn't matter.

Together, they climb a wooden staircase that leads into the room on the second floor where both of the editors are at work.

FERRAND There's nothing to worry about, you'll see. I'm sure you'll be able to make your plane.

They enter the cutting room.

FERRAND Good afternoon, Yann, Martine![1] Have you got the pool sequence loaded and ready?

YANN It's ready to roll.

FERRAND Good. Let's have a look!

The four group themselves around the Moritone.[2]

[1. These roles are played by Yann Dedet and Martine Barraqué, the actual editors of *Day for Night*.]

[2. Moritone is the trade name for an editing machine. In the U.S. they usually are referred to by the generic name of "moviola" (although this is a trademarked name as well). An editing machine enables one to watch the film through a viewer and to listen to the recorded sound simultaneously in order to facilitate editing. The motion and speed can be controled as well.]

On the tiny screen of the Moritone we view the scene shot beside the swimming pool. FERRAND *has forgotten his earlier anger at* STACEY *and congratulates her warmly.*

FERRAND See, Stacey, it doesn't show at all!

STACEY So much the better!

Upon the Moritone we see STACEY *in a bathing suit coming out of the water. Her back is to the camera. She walks toward* ALEXANDRE.

STACEY *(laughing)* You'll just have to put up with me, that's all! It's not *too* evident.

FERRAND From this angle it's not evident at all. It's fine, Stacey. So now you can leave us with your mind at rest.

STACEY *kisses everyone and departs hurriedly. After all, she still has that plane to catch.*

[FERRAND, *suddenly all business, no longer the charming courtier, sets to work with his two film editors.*]

FERRAND *(off-camera)* O.K. That's over with! Let's see the rest!

YANN *presses the button, and the frozen image on the Moritone screen comes to life once more.*

[*The camera pans from the Moritone across the cutting table, Yards and yards of film unreel in colorful coils of orange and black. The sprightly Vivaldi-like theme surges up in the background.*]

VICTORINE. SET: THE ILLICIT BUNGALOW.
EXTERIOR. DAY.

The film unit is shooting on another part of the studio lot today. The exterior set represents a bungalow. We can easily recognize the sketch that DAMIEN, *the art director, showed* FERRAND *for his approval earlier.*

ALPHONSE *and* LILIANE *arrive, tenderly clinging to each other. Quite evidently, they have made up during the previous night.*

ALPHONSE   You know something, Liliane? What I love most is to feel you all over!

He gently caresses her breasts with the palm of his hand. They kiss.

ALPHONSE (*looking around*)   What's this supposed to be?

LILIANE   The bungalow where the lovers—listen, it's all in the script!

ALPHONSE   You know very well I never read scripts!

LILIANE   Well, it's right after Alexandre has taken off with his daughter-in-law. They've just arrived at this place, a motel sort of, that specializes in a certain kind of clientele, if you know what I mean. Anyway, it's morning. They'd like to make love. So, in order not to be bothered by the chambermaid, Pamela sets their breakfast tray down outside the door. Listen, I've got to run. They'll be needing me. Anyway, why don't you take the morning off? You're not needed in this scene.

ALPHONSE   I think I'll hang around, all the same.

LILIANE *leaves* ALPHONSE *and heads in the direction of the technical crew.* ALPHONSE *remains for a moment, lost in thought, staring at her. Then, noticing* JEAN-FRANÇOIS *making off somewhere, he intercepts him, [almost throwing the assistant director off balance].*

ALPHONSE   Jean-François!

JEAN-FRANÇOIS (*trying to break away*)   What is it?

ALPHONSE   There's something I want your opinion about. Are women magical creatures?

JEAN-FRANÇOIS (*dashing off*)   No. Women are not magical creatures. And men aren't, either. Whenever you meet up with a broad who tells you, "I've known some exceptional men," what she really means is, "I've laid a lot of guys."

Standing outside the bungalow, WALTER *has informed* FERRAND *they can proceed with the "serious rehearsal" any time. Just as* FERRAND *is about to give the signal, a young* GRIP[1] *approaches him and asks to see him in private. The two men go off a little way from the rest of the crew. [As they do,* FERRAND *suddenly turns, startled, upon hearing a kitten's cry, off-camera.]*

GRIP Sir, I wanted to ask you if I might take three days off.

FERRAND What? You want to leave the shooting?

GRIP No, sir—I mean—well, my mother just died. . . .

FERRAND Oh, I see. Did it happen all of a sudden?

GRIP No, she'd been suffering a long time. For her, anyway, it was a deliverance.

FERRAND I understand. Certainly. Take three days off.

GRIP Don't worry, sir. I'm seeing that someone will replace me.

The noise of a passing plane drowns out the rest of their conversation. [We can see, though, that FERRAND *is very sympathetic to the young man's obvious unease. They both return to where the crew have been standing around, waiting.]*

Now, everything seems ready. Except that DOCTOR NELSON *has just arrived to say a hurried goodbye to* JULIE, *since his plane is leaving in two hours.* FERRAND, *[the soul of patience,] notices the doctor and tells him to remain if he so wishes: his presence is not at all bothersome on the set.* ODILE, *the make-up girl, gives up her chair, alongside the camera, to* DOCTOR NELSON.

FERRAND (*to* JOELLE) We seem to be ready at long last. I'd like to know why we still haven't begun!

JOELLE We're waiting for Bernard now. As usual!

Inside the bungalow set ALEXANDRE *and* JULIE *are in costume: she wears a nightdress and he a dressing gown.* BERNARD *finally arrives and pours a little bit of milk into a saucer on the breakfast tray.*

BERNARD (*winking at* ALEXANDRE) The milk . . . the antidote.

[1. A grip is a stagehand attached to the camera crew for handling and moving equipment.]

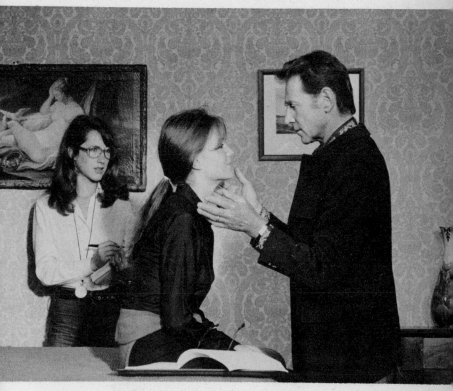

Nathalie Baye, Jacqueline Bisset, Jean-Pierre Aumont, rehearsing before the scene with the cat.

Where there is a poison, there must also be an antidote! (*in English*) I'm ready![1]

Finally, at long last, shooting begins. By this time FERRAND *has decided to dispense with the "serious rehearsal" and shoot an actual take.*

The camera remains outside the window of the bungalow. We can make out ALEXANDRE *and* JULIE *embracing on the edge of the bed.*

FERRAND (*off-camera*) Remember, Alexandre, don't make the kiss too romantic!

The two actors separate. JULIE *takes the breakfast tray and disappears from view. The camera pans down toward the outside door.* JULIE *sets the tray on the cement walk, then shuts the door and reenters the bungalow.*

FERRAND (*off-camera*) Send in the cat!

The crew, motionless, silent, watch as BERNARD *opens a wicker basket and takes out a tiny cat. Despite* BERNARD's *whispered encouragements, the cat refuses to go over to the breakfast tray. It runs in every direction except that one.* BERNARD *is already cursing.*

The take is ruined. It will have to be shot again.

Twice, three times, five times—the cat refuses to go near the tray; or, if it does, it sniffs around vaguely, then scoots off.

Everyone on the set grows tense.

At the outset, with a certain insincerity, FERRAND *had placed all the blame on the poor soundman holding his mike boom just outside the camera range.*

FERRAND It's all your fault, Yorick![2] Take away that silly mike

---

[1. We learn later that BERNARD is a movie buff. Therefore, this is an obvious reference to two Hitchcock films: *Suspicion* (1941) and *Notorious* (1946). In the former, Joan Fontaine wrongly suspected her husband Cary Grant of poisoning her milk. In the latter, Ingrid Bergman was indeed being slowly poisoned by husband Claude Rains by means of milk and cocoa.]

[2. The name of the assistant soundman on *Day for Night,* who here plays the sound engineer, is Harrik Maury. One can assume that

The prop man (Bernard Menez) and the little cat.

on its fishpole! You've scared the poor creature! We don't need sound for this shot!

[*Another crew member jokingly comments that they can dub in all the "wild tracks" of cat meows they need later on at the Nice fish market.*]

The soundman goes off grumbling, mumbling he knows what he'd like to do with his fishpole—but, of course, not quite loud enough for FERRAND *to hear.*

Now, after the fifth spoiled take, it's with BERNARD *that* FERRAND *picks a quarrel.*

FERRAND Listen, it's very simple. We'll stop and begin shooting again when you find me a cat who knows how to act!

BERNARD I don't get it! He should have run straight for the saucer! He hasn't been fed for three days!

JOELLE I told you to bring two cats, Bernard! That way we could have been covered!

JOELLE *dashes off.*

BERNARD (*muttering*) That Joelle's bitchier to me than all the other broads around here combined!

DOCTOR NELSON *profits from the suspended shooting to go over to the open window to talk with* JULIE.

JULIE (*in English*) I'm sorry you're leaving.

NELSON (*in English*) So am I!

ALEXANDRE *comes over, too, and offers to drive* NELSON *to the airport "if we ever manage to wrap up this scene in time." It seems he, too, must get to the airport this afternoon.*

During NELSON *and* ALEXANDRE's *conversation we see* JULIE *take out of her handbag an oblong leather case, which she slides surreptitiously into her husband's left jacket pocket.*

Suddenly JOELLE *arrives—carrying a rather scruffy-looking cat she has "borrowed" from the studio watchman.*

BERNARD You've only to look at his head to see he won't do it! It's not worth wasting film sending him out!

---

when FERRAND calls him "Yorick" he is making a pun on "Harrik" and on that dead "fellow of infinite jest" in the last act of *Hamlet*.]

FERRAND Enough arguing! We'll "screen-test" the studio cat!

They begin shooting once more.

This time everything works perfectly: the cat heads for the break-fast tray, rummages about among the plates and cups, and ends by happily lapping up all the milk in the saucer. FERRAND *allows the shot to run on longer than he had originally planned, so taken is he by the cat's performance. He finally resigns himself to call out: "Cut!"*

The crew, which had held its collective breath during the past two minutes, now breaks out in happy chattering. [The humble studio cat has become the "star" of the day.][1]

A short while later, not far from the huge empty standing set of the Parisian square, a chauffeured limousine awaits ALEXANDRE *and* DOCTOR NELSON. ALPHONSE, *who happens to be passing by, stops* ALEXANDRE.

ALPHONSE Excuse me for bothering you, Alexandre, I realize you're in a hurry, but I have only one little question to ask you.

ALEXANDRE Yes?

ALPHONSE In your opinion, are women magical creatures?

ALEXANDRE *(smiling)* Some of them, yes! Others—no!

And ALEXANDRE *catches up with* DOCTOR NELSON. [ALPHONSE *goes over and shakes the doctor's hand, wishing him a good trip.*]

The two men climb into the back seat of the limousine. The car drives off.

Inside the car [back projection of the suburbs of Nice behind the two men]:

ALEXANDRE You know, Doctor, you can set your mind at ease concerning Julie.

[1. In *Soft Skin,* a middle-aged writer (Jean Desailly) and his young mistress (Françoise Dorléac) make love early in the morning at a bungalow similar to this one. At the end of the scene the young woman sets a breakfast tray outside the door, and a cat comes to hunt in it for scraps of food. One wonders if Truffaut's troubles with a recalcitrant cat at that time inspired this sequence nine years later.]

NELSON Yes, I realize that. She's very happy making this film. I'm sure she won't let anything upset her.

ALEXANDRE It's amazing, isn't it, how vulnerable we actors are!

NELSON It's very normal. Everyone is afraid of being judged—but in your profession that judgment is a part of your daily round, not only in your work but in your private life as well.

ALEXANDRE As soon as we actors meet someone, we ask ourselves: "What does he think of me? Does he like me?" Oh, but I think it's the same for all artists! When Mozart was a child and people asked him to play, he would answer: "I'll play for you whatever you wish—but first tell me that you love me!"

While listening to ALEXANDRE, NELSON *has mechanically put one hand in his jacket pocket. He finds the leather box* JULIE *had slipped in there earlier. He opens it and smiles, looking at the gift it contains [a silver watch-fob that also resembles a handcuff, if one wishes to be symbolical].*

NELSON And then, too, it's the profession where people kiss each other the most. . . .

ALEXANDRE You've noticed that already, have you? Yes, we spend half our time kissing each other. I've heard that the handshake was invented in order for men to prove to one another that they were not carrying weapons, that they were not foes. But for us that's not enough. We must show that we *love* each other as well! *"Mon chéri . . . (in English)* my darling . . . my love . . . you are magnificent!" *(in French once more)* We seem somehow to need that. . . .

The limousine pulls up in front of the Nice Airport. The two men get out and go their separate ways, after shaking hands.

While DOCTOR NELSON *heads for the departure gate,* ALEXANDRE *[after checking the time on a large digital clock in the main lobby] heads toward the arrival gate. [He is wearing dark glasses now.]*

[Suddenly he takes off his glasses, his face lighting up.] A very tanned, handsome, dark-haired young man breaks away from the group of people just coming through the gate and walks over to him.

*[*ALEXANDRE *and the handsome young man walk away together, arm in arm. The image freezes upon them.]*

[*Cut to a red light above a soundstage door. The sign* NO ADMITTANCE: SHOOTING IN PROGRESS *suddenly goes out.*]

VICTORINE STUDIOS. EXTERIOR. LATE AFTERNOON.

The crew of Meet Pamela *is leaving at the end of the day's shooting. The young man whom* ALEXANDRE *had met at the airport stands waiting outside the door of the soundstage.* ALEXANDRE *exits, and introduces him to various people.*

ALEXANDRE (*to* FERRAND) I'd like you to meet Christian Fersen.[1] (*to* CHRISTIAN) Our director, Monsieur Ferrand.

FERRAND Were you waiting here a long time? You could have come in to watch the shooting. There's nothing secret about it, you know!

Not far away, BERNARD *has observed the scene. He makes a leering face at* ALPHONSE.

BERNARD Well, I'll be goddamned! Do you see what I see!

But ALPHONSE *has other preoccupations at the moment. He puts to the prop man "the eternal question"—since no answer has yet satisfied him.*

ALPHONSE Tell me, Bernard, are women magical creatures?

BERNARD What? No. Not at all! Well, their legs are magical maybe. Why else is it we guys wear the pants and they the skirts?

He is interrupted by LILIANE.

LILIANE Oh, print it and can it, the two of you! You never seem to talk about anything else! Tell me, Alphonse, are we going to the movies again tonight, or what?

ALPHONSE Of course, we're going to the movies!

[1. The name of Alexandre's young lover will remind some of that of Marie Antoinette's dashing Danish nobleman lover, Count Hans Axel Fersen.]

JOELLE *has just come out of the soundstage.*

LILIANE Oh, Joelle, do you know what time the movie starts?

JOELLE Right away. In fact, if we don't want to miss the credits, we'd better hurry.

A short distance away, the producer BERTRAND *has just rushed up to* FERRAND.

BERTRAND I just got the news, Ferrand. The night shooting in the kitchen scene has to be done tomorrow evening, without fail. The set workers have to have at least a twelve-hour break between work periods, you see. It's in their union contract.

FERRAND *isn't overjoyed by this bit of news. He gestures to* JOELLE, *who comes over.*

FERRAND It looks like we'll have to shoot the kitchen scene tomorrow.

JOELLE What? Tomorrow night?

FERRAND Yes. So you'll have to work with me on the script tonight.

JOELLE O.K. (*she returns to the others*) Sorry, kids, I can't go to the movies with you.

ALPHONSE Well, we'll just have to get along without you!

JULIE *has overheard part of the conversation. She calls* FERRAND *in turn.*

JULIE Ferrand, about that scene in the kitchen . . .

FERRAND Yes, Julie, we have to shoot it tomorrow night, as a matter of fact.

JULIE I'd like to have my lines.

FERRAND Yes. We'll give them to you tonight, right after dinner.

JULIE Oh, that's cutting it very close . . .

FERRAND I realize that. But the scene hasn't been written yet, you know. Listen to me, Julie: you can read it once before going to sleep, then put it under your pillow. I wager that tomorrow morning you'll have a wonderful surprise: you'll know it all by heart!

JULIE (*smiling, to* FERRAND *who is already dashing off*) Optimist!

Hotel Atlantic. Interior. Night.

This evening BERTRAND *is dining alone with* JULIE *in the hotel dining room. He has already embarked upon a long speech which he obviously knows by heart.*

BERTRAND Reporters are all alike. They always ask the same questions: "How does it feel to be famous? How do you react when people ask you for autographs? When people recognize you on the street?" In all the many television programs I've seen about moviemaking, I've yet to see one which shows that an actress, whenever she's working on a film, must get up at six each morning—or that she never gets home before nine each night. Think of it: a total of fifteen hours a day spent working!

JULIE (*mischievously*) Oh, surely not fifteen! Thirteen . . . fourteen, maybe? If one counts the time watching rushes?

Ferrand's Hotel Room. Interior. Night.

FERRAND, *seated on the edge of the bed, scans a newspaper which he has opened to the movie page.*

FERRAND At the Kursaal: *The Godfather.* At the Rexy: *The Godfather.*[1] Look at this: *The Godfather's* everywhere! You'd think no other films had been made lately!

[1. The choice of "Kursaal" and "Rexy" is a joke. No such theaters exist in Nice. "Kursaal" also happens to be the name of the café-nightclub in the opening sequence of Fellini's *I Vitelloni* (1953).]

He has stood up while speaking. He now comes alongside
JOELLE, *who is seated in front of a typewriter.*

JOELLE Speaking of godfathers—and godsons—did you see the
boy Alexandre had been waiting for ever since shooting started?
That Alexandre fooled everybody, didn't he? Here we'd all been
expecting some cute little Lolita—and it's a handsome young
Lorenzaccio who finally gets off the plane! You know, I've just
thought of something. Why couldn't we use him to double for
Pamela in the auto accident sequence?[1]

FERRAND You're out of your mind! That's a dangerous job! We'll
have to get a real stuntman to do it. . . . O.K. Let's get back
to the kitchen! Now then, it's the middle of the night. Alexandre comes upon his daughter-in-law in the kitchen. What
next?

JOELLE I don't even understand *why* the kitchen!

FERRAND It can only work in the kitchen. You see, don't you, we
have to avoid anything suspicious at all costs. Now here's part of
a first draft I started, but I'm not at all happy with it.

FERRAND *hands some sheets of paper to* JOELLE, *who quickly
scans them.*

JOELLE (*reading aloud*) "Alexandre: You know what's happening to us, don't you?" "Pamela: I think so."

JOELLE *sets the sheets of paper down on the table.*

JOELLE "I think so. . ." No, that's very bad. Pamela isn't vague.
She must be certain by this time that she's in love with her
father-in-law. Otherwise, she's too spineless. No, if you ask
me, this scene won't work at all. There's something missing—
a central idea. Why don't you telephone the original scriptwriter, Jean Marius, to help you?

[1. *Lorenzaccio* is a play by Alfred de Musset, known to most cultured
Frenchmen, and therefore the nickname JOELLE chooses here will
seem more subtly disturbing in a subconscious manner to them than it
might to American audiences. In Musset's play Duke Alessandro de'
Medici ("Alexandre" in French) is killed by his younger cousin
Lorenzino (or "Lorenzaccio"). The choice of Lorenzaccio here, and
all that talk about an auto accident, is just one more example of how
Truffaut casually "throws away" material which a lesser artist would
emphasize with all the stops pulled out.]

FERRAND Believe me, I've thought of that. But he's not in Paris right now, he's in Japan. He's working on an adaptation of Turgenev's *First Love,* with the setting changed to modern Japan. It's an interesting idea.

FERRAND *has stood up once more. He takes the tray containing the remnants of his and* JOELLE's *evening meal and sets it down on the bed.*

FERRAND Anyway, it's better idea than *Meet Pamela!* I'd have done better to shoot that! Although, when you come right down to it, you can make a film out of almost anything!

FERRAND *has taken up the* Nice-Matin *and he scans the headlines.*

FERRAND You could make movies out of any of these: KISSINGER'S FRUITFUL MISSION. A HEART TRANSPLANT. JEWELER SHOOTS WIFE.

JOELLE O.K., old buddy, let's get back to the kitchen, huh? You dictate and I'll type. Don't forget you promised to give Julie her lines tonight!

FERRAND *returns to sit down alongside the table.*

FERRAND Now, let's see—the kitchen. We must steer clear of anything that might seem sneaky or shameful. These two characters know quite well what they're doing. They're conscious of their actions. They accept the idea that they must leave this house like thieves in the night. . . .

JOELLE As a matter of fact, you might have Pamela say exactly that: "Let's leave like thieves in the night"! I think that in this scene we must show in the most absolute way Pamela's complete lucidity: she loved the son, she loves him no longer, she is now madly in love with the father. It's absolutely necessary that the audience understand her feelings.

FERRAND I agree. What's more, it was very well put by Julie herself. Just read the interview she gave at the airport in the *Nice-Matin.* (*he reads*) "Meet Pamela is the story of a young woman who realizes that the boy she married is but a pale reflection of his father . . . and that the truly remarkable individual is the

The director and the script girl hard at work (François Truffaut and Nathalie Baye).
"O.K., old buddy, back to work! You dictate and I'll type . . ."

father." That's it, exactly! Julie is the only one thus far to have understood the script![1]

JOELLE Yes, I see.

FERRAND And do you know why? Quite obviously, because Julie's mother was a celebrated actress—but also because she grew up in Hollywood, and Hollywood is full of children who struggle to equal their famous parents: the Fairbanks, the Barrymores, that whole crowd. (*he dictates*) "Alexandre: You know what's happening to us, don't you?"

The telephone rings.

FERRAND Oh, shit! (*lifts the receiver*) Hello?

HOTEL CLERK (*voice-off*) Monsieur Ferrand, there's a Mademoiselle Dominique here. Should I send her up?

FERRAND No. Please tell her I'm very sorry, but I have to work tonight. I'll telephone her tomorrow.

HOTEL ATLANTIC LOBBY. INTERIOR. NIGHT.

The desk clerk hangs up the receiver and turns to face a pretty young woman who stands, waiting.

DESK CLERK Monsieur Ferrand is very sorry, mademoiselle, but he has not finished working. He can't see you this evening. He will telephone you tomorrow.

[1. The interview at the Nice Airport, as filmed, contains no such comment by JULIE. We are faced with two possibilities here: Either what we viewed of the press conference earlier was an *edited* version of a much longer interview; or some reporter, in filing his story for the *Nice-Matin,* "expanded" JULIE BAKER's own words in order to make for more interesting copy. If the latter is so, then Truffaut the filmmaker is being doubly ironic: for it was the reporter then, and not JULIE BAKER, who truly "understood the script"!]

YOUNG WOMAN (*smiling*) Thank you. Good night!

BERNARD *and* JEAN-FRANÇOIS *have been watching the scene. They comment upon the young woman as she exits from the lobby.*

BERNARD You tell me. What do you make of it?

JEAN-FRANÇOIS Succulent . . . *very* succulent!

BERNARD A beauty of the region?

JEAN-FRANÇOIS A local call-girl?

BERNARD Oh, no, I disagree!

JEAN-FRANÇOIS "The warrior's rest" then?[1]

BERNARD You know, that's exactly what I was going to say!

At this moment we hear the voice of PIERRE TCHERNIA *coming from the television set in the lobby.* [PIERRE TCHERNIA *is the host of a very popular French TV quiz show,* Monsieur Cinéma.]

TCHERNIA (*voice-off*) In what film was Jeanne Moreau the Empress of Russia?

JEAN-FRANÇOIS Hey, it's that movie quiz. Come over here, Bernard!

Both men go to stand in front of the television set.

JEAN-FRANÇOIS *The Great Catherine.*[2]

CONTESTANT (*voice-off*) *The Great Catherine.*

TCHERNIA (*voice-off*) Very good! Now, in what film was Jeanne Moreau the partner of Orson Welles and also an interpreter of Shakespeare?

BERNARD Easy . . . that's easy. . . .

[1. The U.S. subtitles translate this very aptly as "Rest and Recreation." But, to these two film buffs, the phrase "Warrior's Rest" would also remind them of the film of the same title, *Le Repos du Guerrier,* starring Brigitte Bardot and Robert Hossein, which Roger Vadim directed in 1962 from Christiane Rochefort's novel.]

[2. *The Great Catherine,* made in 1968, was directed by Gordon Flemyng, and also starred Peter O'Toole. It is one of Jeanne Moreau's few English-language films.]

JEAN-FRANÇOIS AND BERNARD (*at the same time*) Falstaff![1]

CONTESTANT (*voice-off*) Falstaff.

TCHERNIA (*voice-off*) Correct. Now, in what film was Jeanne Moreau the sister of Charles IX and the wife of the king of Navarre?

BERNARD Oh, shit, it's—it's that thingamajig about Henri IV.

JEAN-FRANÇOIS *La Reine Margot.*[2]

CONTESTANT (*voice-off*) *La Reine Margot.*

BERNARD Just what I was about to say!

TCHERNIA (*voice-off*) You certainly know a lot about films!

JULIE'S HOTEL ROOM. INTERIOR. NIGHT.

JOELLE *slides a sheet of paper under the door [and calls out softly: "Here are your lines for the kitchen scene, Julie!"]*

JULIE *walks over to pick them up, then takes them with her into the bathroom. She sets the paper up against the mirror. As she begins removing her make-up, piling her hair on top of her head, she reads aloud.*

[1. *Falstaff* (also known as *Chimes at Midnight*) was directed by Orson Welles and finally released in 1966, after nearly two calamitous years of shooting, reshooting, and editing. It also starred Keith Baxter, Margaret Rutherford, and John Gielgud.]

[2. *La Reine Margot,* directed by Jean Dréville in 1954, was an unsuccessful fustian melodrama, in which Françoise Rosay played Catherine de' Medici. Another question Tchernia might have asked: "Name three films directed by François Truffaut in which Jeanne Moreau has appeared." *The Four Hundred Blows* (in a guest bit), *Jules and Jim,* and *The Bride Wore Black.* She also appeared in her ex-husband Jean-Louis Richard's *Mata Hari,* for which Truffaut wrote the dialogue.]

JULIE "Yes. I'm in love with you. . . . The same time as you. Since the fancy-dress ball. . . . I can no longer remain here. I've decided to leave tomorrow. . . ."

VICTORINE STUDIOS. EXTERIOR. NIGHT.

It is late at night. But for once the lot is not quiet. The kind of agitation that always precedes the shooting of a sequence reigns everywhere.

We are outside the set of the parents' villa [which we saw earlier in broad daylight in the scene where ALPHONSE *brought his young wife to meet his mother and father]. On the curving stone steps that lead up to the main entrance electricians are adjusting various lights, under the direction of the head gaffer.* WALTER, *the director of photography, and his assistant camera-man have set up the camera on a movable platform. Through the lighted window of the kitchen set we can see* JULIE *rehearsing her movements about the room.*

ALEXANDRE *has been sitting down on the lawn below, watching all the preparations, the picture of calm. He now gets up and walks up the steps to join* JULIE *in the kitchen.*

Outside the open kitchen window, BERNARD *checks the installation of the pipes that will allow water to stream down before the façade. On the platform* WALTER *and his camera operator are ready to begin shooting. But everything inside the set is still chaos. We see* JEAN-FRANÇOIS *fussing about setting a bouquet of flowers on top of the refrigerator, moving it about and checking how it will appear behind the two characters when viewed through the window.*

FERRAND, *who is in the kitchen, whispers something to* JOELLE. *She rushes down the villa steps on some errand or other.*

CHRISTIAN FERSEN *goes over and sits down in the chair vacated earlier by* ALEXANDRE.

FERRAND *shuts the kitchen window and gives last-minute instructions to his two actors.*

FERRAND The main thing is not to play the scene sentimentally. Be hard, slightly brutal. Even a bit violent, as you rehearsed it earlier. That went very well.

FERRAND *leaves the kitchen and goes over to stand on the platform alongside the camera.* WALTER *calls out, "Ready!" and* JOELLE *holds up the clapboard through the kitchen window.*

BERNARD *begins the false rain, regulating its flow according to* WALTER's *indications.*

At the start of the scene, JULIE *is alone in the shadows. She has just entered, walking over to open the refrigerator in the dark kitchen to pour herself a glass of milk. She walks over to the window, stares out. The rain trickles down the pane before her face. Suddenly the kitchen light comes on. We can make out* ALEXANDRE *in the background.*

JULIE-PAMELA "You weren't asleep?"

ALEXANDRE "No. I heard someone moving about in here. I knew it was you. You weren't able to sleep, either?"

JULIE-PAMELA "I was thinking about you."

ALEXANDRE "You know what's happened to us, don't you?"

JULIE-PAMELA "Yes. I'm in love with you."

ALEXANDRE "When did you know?"

JULIE-PAMELA "The same time as you. Since the fancy-dress ball. I can no longer remain here. I've decided to leave tomorrow."

ALEXANDRE "I've thought about that, too. But I'd rather we both left together."

JULIE-PAMELA "No. I must leave alone. If we went off together, it would be like running away, eloping."

ALEXANDRE "It will seem like an elopement, no matter how we do it. I don't want to lose you."

JULIE-PAMELA "Nor I you. Let's leave right now then. Like thieves in the night."

The voices of the actors have a quality of emotion that seems even more heightened by the dark rain-filled silence surround-

François Truffaut directs Jacqueline Bisset.

ing them. We could almost believe that we were watching a real-life drama between JULIE *and* ALEXANDRE. *In the viewfinder of the camera, we see their two tiny silhouettes which suddenly go rigid as* FERRAND's *voice calls out,* "Cut!"

[*The shutter of the camera begins to close over the scene, as it did earlier at the end of the ruined take where* SÉVERINE *became hysterical while* ALEXANDRE *held her in his arms. Only this time the "wipe effect" begins at the lower right-hand corner of the screen and moves up diagonally, not horizontally. Finally the entire screen is black.*]

HOTEL ATLANTIC. FERRAND'S ROOM. INTERIOR. NIGHT.

Later, that same night. FERRAND *has a hard time falling asleep. He hears* JULIE's *voice, repeating over and over:* "Let's leave right now . . . like thieves in the night . . . let's leave right now. . ."

Finally, when he does fall asleep, the little boy carrying the long cane walks once more in his dreams. He comes tap-tap-tapping down the same deserted street [*the shot still black and white on color stock*].

[*This time the boy gets a little further in his journey. He comes smack up against some iron grille gates—but before we can make out what is behind them the camera has cut to a bright color shot of the tall white wooden gates of the Victorine Studios, shining in the morning sunlight.*]

Victorine Studios. Exterior. Day.

At the far end of the huge standing set of the Parisian square the technical crew bustle about the camera.

In the foreground, [framed in an open door,] ALPHONSE and FERRAND are having it out with each other.

FERRAND Why is it, old buddy, you're never around when we need you? We've been hunting all over for you for over an hour!

ALPHONSE I was in my dressing room. All anyone had to do was come up and get me.

FERRAND But you were told last night you'd be needed here on the set this morning!

ALPHONSE *makes a sign for* FERRAND *to lower his voice.*

ALPHONSE If I knew what was expected of me, I would certainly do it! But I wasn't even given a work schedule!

FERRAND All right. Let's not waste any more time arguing. There's work to be done.

They move off, into the bright sunlight, heading toward the camera crew.

We are now in back of the huge standing set. [The flats look very ramshackle viewed from this angle.] FERRAND and JEAN-FRANÇOIS come toward the camera, thumbing through the thick red-covered script, talking animatedly. We cannot hear their words.

FERRAND *(voice-over)* Here we are now in the middle of our adventure. Before beginning to shoot a film, I want above all to make a movie that will be beautiful. As soon as the first storms appear on the horizon I lower my sights. I hope, simply, to be able to finish the film, period.

Toward the middle of shooting, I always make an examination of conscience. I berate myself: "You should have worked harder, you should have given of yourself more. . . ." Oh well, I think. There still remains the second half in which to recoup my losses. And, starting from that moment, I struggle more than ever to make whatever finally appears on the screen come more alive.

Meet Pamela seems to be on the right track—at last. The actors appear comfortable in their characters, the crew is a well-knit group, personal problems no longer count. Cinema rules the day!

Music rises in the background, growing more and more powerful, accompanying two and one half minutes of isolated images, all designed to illustrate shooting a film, the passage of time, work in progress:[1]

Shooting, this time in close-up, a conversation between ALPHONSE *and* JULIE-PAMELA. FERRAND *goes over to show* JULIE *how to hold her head high, using her neck for an axis when she turns away from* ALPHONSE.

The red light over a soundstage door goes on.

ALPHONSE *advances, reciting lines we cannot hear. His gait is odd; and as the camera pulls away we learn why. He must carefully lift each foot over the crossties of the track upon which a camera recedes as he walks toward it.*

FERRAND *shows* JULIE *exactly how to place her fingers upon a window sill so that her gesture will be extremely stylized.*

Another red light goes on.

An electrician, with the help of a panel swung back and forth before a spotlight, gives the illusion of a door opening and closing upon ALEXANDRE's *face.*

An exterior sequence, during which the camera pans rapidly while following ALPHONSE *and* JULIE. *The technical crew is forced to crouch down on the ground in order not to be within the camera's range.*

SÉVERINE *shakes out her hair, laughing all the while.*

---

1. This phrase in English in the original script.

In SÉVERINE's *dressing room, a script in hand,* ODILE *helps the Italian actress learn her lines.*

While waiting for a scene to begin, SÉVERINE *and* ODILE *enjoy a good laugh together.*

SÉVERINE *and* JULIE *stand over a group of contact prints attached to a board. With a wax pencil they x out those which displease them.* [SÉVERINE *points out to* JULIE *how lovely she looks in one of them and then makes a great pantomimic show of how ugly she herself appears in all of them.*]

FERRAND *calls out,* "Camera!" [*although we do not hear the sound*]. LILIANE *steps up and holds the clapboard before* ALPHONSE, *whose face is hidden behind a newspaper.*

JOELLE, *holding a chronometer, times a take.*

The red light goes out.

In one corner of the lot an enormous statue of Lincoln appears, moving as if of its own accord. Then we see BERNARD, *driving a small electric handcar, which has been towing the statue.*

ALPHONSE *and* JULIE *are seated in the front seat of the blue convertible. The camera has been set up in the back trunk.* FERRAND *holds up the clapboard, then crouches down in the back seat of the convertible. The car starts off.*

ALPHONSE, *again with* JULIE *beside him, drives the convertible, which is attached to a truck traveling ahead of it, upon which the camera is placed.* [JULIE *herself holds the clapboard this time.*]

FERRAND, *standing alongside the camera on the truck, gives instructions to the two actors in the convertible.* JULIE *lights a cigarette, hands it to* ALPHONSE. *A few moments later, following* FERRAND's *cue,* ALPHONSE *tosses the cigarette away.*

The same scene in the convertible is shot in broad daylight, then at night.

We see pass in front of us the strange tandem of the traveling truck and the blue convertible. It is dusk. Spotlights have been set up on the truck, diffusing light within the convertible. The entire technical crew huddles as best it can upon the platform on the traveling truck.

A night sequence is being shot on the Parisian square.

An arc light suddenly comes on.

The platform holding the camera and its operators swings up toward a window on one of the façades. As soon as this crane shot ends, we hear BERNARD'S *voice:*

BERNARD Don't run away, everybody! Tonight the drinks are on Alexandre!

And thus the 150-second set piece on shooting Meet Pamela *comes to an end. [The music, until now elegiac, fades into the* bal musette *accordion theme we heard briefly at the end of the credits.]*

VICTORINE. THE STUDIO BAR. EXTERIOR. NIGHT.

A buffet has been set up beneath some trees adjacent to the Victorine bar.

BERNARD *arrives, carrying a tray of sandwiches and a bottle of* pastis.[1]

ALEXANDRE What? Isn't there any more champagne?

BERNARD I only got three bottles. So we'll have to start pushing *pastis.*

The entire crew is present. ALEXANDRE *encourages everyone to drink. He pours a glass of champagne from what little is left and then takes it over to* SÉVERINE, *who is deep in conversation with* CHRISTIAN FERSEN. ALEXANDRE *leads* SÉVERINE *away.*

SÉVERINE (*after a final glance at* CHRISTIAN) You know, he's very handsome! Does he want to be in films?

[1. *Pastis* is an apéritif made out of anise, very popular throughout France, but especially so in the south.]

ALEXANDRE In films? Oh, no, God forbid! He's doing very well with his tennis, you know.

SÉVERINE Well then, *auguri* . . . ! [my best wishes to him . . . !]

ALEXANDRE As a matter of fact, there's something concerning Christian I wanted to ask your opinion about. You see, I've decided to adopt him. I've always dreamed of having a son, you know, and then—but you'll probably think me an idiot to say this!—I'd like to feel that after I'm dead someone was carrying on my name.[1]

SÉVERINE Why, it's a wonderful idea!

ALEXANDRE Do you think so? But there are some difficulties— difficulties in the legal aspect, I mean. You see, I'm no longer married—and Christian doesn't have a French passport.

SÉVERINE You know what I'd do if I were you? I'd speak to President Lebaye.[2]

In a corner two children sit at a table playing "Seven Families" [a card game similar to the American "Fish"].

LITTLE GIRL Do you have a grandfather in the "Electrician Family"?

LITTE BOY No. Fish! Do you have a mother in the "Cameraman Family"?

[It is quite obvious from their choice of "families" (for the "seven families" in the actual game do not include "electricians" and "cameramen") that these two kids are the offspring of technical crew members.]

[1. One cannot help but be reminded here of Jean Cocteau (whom Truffaut has often spoken of admiringly). Cocteau legally adopted Edouard Dermit, the young gardener whom he first made an actor in *The Eagle Has Two Heads* (1947) and who is now heir to his vast estate. There is also the case of another of Cocteau's protegés, Jean Marais, adopting a young man whom Marais claimed (causing much journalistic skepticism) to have been the actual father of. Perhaps one is reading too much into coincidences to note here that the name Truffaut earlier gave to the original scriptwriter of *Meet Pamela* was "Jean Marius."]

[2. An imaginary name, according to Truffaut himself.]

While SÉVERINE *explains her idea to* ALEXANDRE *concerning* CHRISTIAN'*s adoption, the drinking continues merrily.* BERNARD *and* ODILE *wander from group to group, offering trays of sandwiches and refilling empty glasses.*

BERTRAND, *a hefty-looking dark-haired young man at his side, seeks out* FERRAND, *who is chatting with* JULIE.

BERTRAND Oh, Ferrand, I'd like you to meet Mark Spencer. He's our English stuntman. Just over from London, in fact. I warn you: don't talk to him in French, for he doesn't understand a single word!

FERRAND Oh, good, then Julie will have to arrange things. Julie, I'd like you to tell him that the auto accident we're shooting tomorrow will be done *en nuit américaine.*

JULIE What does that mean—*nuit américaine?*

FERRAND It's when you shoot a night scene, but in broad daylight. You know, by putting a filter in front of the lens.

JULIE (*In English*) Oh, "day for night." It's called "day for night" in English.[1]

FERRAND Is that so? Oh, good!

JULIE (*to the stuntman, in English*) They're going to shoot tomorrow's scene "day for night."

STUNTMAN (*in English*) Who am I doubling, do you know?

JULIE (*laughing, turning to Ferrand*) He just asked me who he's going to double!

FERRAND (*pointing to her*) Julie!

STUNTMAN (*in English*) Oh, very nice! In that?

[JULIE *is wearing a long-skirted orange dress, with many ruffles, and a rather low-cut bodice.*]

FERRAND (*in French*) Yes, exactly like that, exactly as she's dressed now!

[1. *La nuit américaine* ("American night") came from the fact that U.S. filmmakers were the first to employ this technique, especially in Westerns. Often, particularly in color films, such sequences possess a strange glimmer which may enhance them poetically but which nevertheless strike the trained eye as unnatural, especially concerning cloud formations and panoramic vistas.]

JULIE (*in English*) With a wig.

STUNTMAN (*to* FERRAND, *in English*) Are you gonna work in England someday?[1]

FERRAND *looks confused, appealing to* JULIE *for help.*

JULIE (*laughing, in French*) It's very amusing—because neither of you understands a word the other one is saying!

FERRAND (*in English*) I speak English very well, but I don't understand it!

They all laugh.

HOTEL ATLANTIC. INTERIOR. DAY.

The next morning. ALPHONSE *remains in bed, since he won't be needed for today's shooting.* LILIANE *rushes about the room, collecting her things.*

[*The hotel room appears changed from the last time we saw it. It now has only one bed in it, as far as we can see. And most of the furniture has been rearranged again.*]

ALPHONSE Tell me now, Liliane. Wouldn't you rather stay here with me for a little while this morning?

LILIANE Are you crazy or something?

ALPHONSE Whatever it is they're shooting today, they won't need you.

LILIANE Yes, they will. They're shooting Pamela's death in the automobile. With the English stuntman.

ALPHONSE You know very well it's not an important scene![2]

[1. Truffaut, of course, shot almost all of *Fahrenheit 451* in England in 1966.]

[2. We've already seen, during the shooting of the bungalow sequence, how ALPHONSE is scornful of the importance of any scene in *Meet Pamela* in which he himself does not take part.]

Dani and Jean-Pierre Léaud.
"I tell you, I have to go. . . !"

LILIANE I tell you, I have to go! What's more, they're waiting outside for me right now!

LILIANE *has been looking out of the window. She finally gathers her script and her notebooks and is about to rush off when she remembers—and comes over to the bed to kiss* ALPHONSE.

LILIANE See you later!

ALPHONSE *suddenly notices the watch on* LILIANE's *wrist, and he holds* LILIANE *tightly, preventing her from leaving.*

ALPHONSE Where did this come from?

LILIANE (*casually*) Oh, it's Pierrot's. He loaned it to me while my own is being repaired.

ALPHONSE Give that photographer his watch back today! I have enough money to buy you another watch if you need one!

They kiss. ALPHONSE's *hand comes down to rest tenderly between* LILIANE's *thighs. She smiles at him.*

LILIANE You're making it hard for me to leave by doing that.

ALPHONSE No, no. Go on to your job. But I'm leaving you my hand—there! I commit it to your care.

LILIANE (*with a knowing look*) Yes, I'll keep it warm there for you. . . .

She rushes out.

In front of the hotel JEAN-FRANÇOIS *hurries about, dispatching the various cars of the crew [as well as the huge equipment vans of the Victorine. There is an air of unaccustomed excitement, as if everyone were departing on that stagecoach trip across the Continental Divide* FERRAND *referred to earlier].*

JEAN-FRANÇOIS O.K., you guys, speed it up, huh? Time's a-wasting! In the saddle, everybody! Ride!

LILIANE *comes out of the lobby and runs over to* ODILE, *who has been waiting for her. Before getting into the car,* LILIANE *looks up at* ALPHONSE, *who is watching the departure from his window two stories above. [*LILIANE *puts the palm of her hand flat against her crotch.] She gives* ALPHONSE *a conspiratorial wink.*

The caravan sets forth.

From her window JULIE *also watches the noisy departure.*

JULIE (*looking across to* ALPHONSE) What are you going to do today?

ALPHONSE And you?

JULIE I thought I'd go up into the hills to look for antiques.

ALPHONSE Oh, I think I'll go to the movies.

A STREET IN NICE. EXTERIOR. DAY.

The procession of trucks and cars rolls down a small side street.

[*In the background we hear, rather humorously, a kind of "wagons westward" music usually associated with American cowboy films.*]

The caravan passes a street sign: RUE JEAN VIGO.[1]

At the outskirts of the city a large sign shaped in the form of an arrow, marked PAMELA, *indicates the direction in which the caravan must proceed. The cars and vans turn left, then right, at last disappearing down a road leading up into the mountainous region behind Nice. Other signs, similarly marked, move past our eyes in various directions.*

[1. There is, indeed, such a street on the outskirts of Nice, not far from the Victorine Studios. Yet it is unlikely that the group would have had to proceed down this tiny street on their way to the location. It is used by Truffaut as an *hommage* to the great French director of *Zero for Conduct* (1933), *L'Atalante* (1934), and, perhaps most fitting of all here, *A Propos de Nice* (1930).

Mountain road. Exterior. Day.

BERNARD, *at the wheel of his car, comes upon* JOELLE, *standing in the middle of the road, making distress signals. He stops the car.*

BERNARD Now what's wrong?

JOELLE Oh, don't be such a pain in the ass! I've got a flat!

BERNARD *has already gotten out of his car. He walks over to* JOELLE's *station wagon.*

BERNARD Well, don't you know how to change a flat?

JOELLE Shut up and help me! We'll be late if we don't hurry!

BERNARD Then give me that.

He takes the crank from JOELLE's *hands, and crouches down alongside the station wagon.*

BERNARD When you're in the driver's seat, and everything's going fine, then you don't need to be nice to somebody like me, do you? But once you're in a jam—!

JOELLE Stop talking and get to work! We'll be late, I tell you!

BERNARD You're some mechanic! You had the jack under the wrong tire! It's the front one that's flat!

While BERNARD *gets busy, a car passes them on the road.*

Finally, the tire is changed. But by now both JOELLE *and* BERNARD *are filthy. They decide to go and wash in the stream that runs parallel to the road in the bushes a few feet below.*

At the water's edge JOELLE *and* BERNARD *wash.* JOELLE *calmly takes off her white blouse. She wears nothing but a bra above her waist.*

BERNARD Er, you know, Joelle, if you wanted to—

JOELLE If I wanted to what?

BERNARD Well, uh, here we are . . . the two of us . . . and all alone . . .

JOELLE I couldn't agree with you more, old buddy!

BERNARD What?

JOELLE Just as I thought! When it comes to handing out a line, there's no one better at it than you. But when it comes to the real thing, there's nobody at home down there!

BERNARD Then you—you really want to?

And quite evidently JOELLE *has made up her mind—for she has already begun taking off her blue jeans.*

JOELLE Sure—but let's not drag it out forever, huh?

She disappears into the bushes, wearing nothing but her panties.

JOELLE (*off-camera*) Come on, hurry up!

BERNARD *follows her. But, before he does, he looks around, dumbstruck. He cannot believe what is happening to him.*

LOCATION SITE. EXTERIOR. DAY.

[*A road sign indicates that the location site is* La Vésubie. *This region, high in the mountains behind Nice, is noted for its scenic gorges—and also for its perilous hairpin turns.*]

The actual location site is a sharp curve in the road. One side of the road is carved out of the mountain, while the other drops steeply over two hundred feet into the valley below, [with the curve itself protected by nothing more than a few stone markers hardly six inches high].

The crew has almost finished setting up its equipment.

FERRAND What could have happened to Joelle?

ASSISTANT CAMERAMAN Bernard's nowhere to be found, either!

On the other side of the curve, JEAN-FRANÇOIS *and* LILIANE *are fussing over the stuntman's costume.* ODILE *is trying to fit*

the short wig on his head. The stuntman's getup (long skirt, low-necked blouse, inflated breasts) has inspired quite a few raunchy remarks, even more to the point than usual, since everyone knows that the fellow does not understand a word of French. LILIANE *is the only one who defends him.*

LILIANE You're all sick! (*to the stuntman, in English*) Give me your watch.

[*When one of the technicians asks* LILIANE *if that's all she wants the stuntman to give her, she explodes:*]

LILIANE You're revolting! If he understood French, he'd make mincemeat out of all of you—and that's exactly what you deserve! Bunch of perverts! Don't you have anything better to do with your time than make dirty jokes?

Coming up the road from the bridge which crosses the ravine a short distance below are two peasants, who add a picturesque note to the proceedings with their donkey and small cart.

PEASANT What do you know! There's some people up here, for a change! You're making a movie, eh? Well, if you need a star, I'm right here, remember!

[*One crew member laughs, making some disparaging remarks about "peasants." Another comments: "We're all of us peasants —Jewish peasants, that is!"[1]*]

Further up the road, PIERROT *the photographer* [*who seems to have been deserted by* LILIANE *these days*] *is standing very close to a pretty young girl bicyclist, whispering intimately into her ear.*

ELECTRICIAN Hey, Pierrot, heard anything from your wife and kids lately?

This classic line causes the crew to break up laughing—all except PIERROT, *of course, whose own "line" has now been cut down most effectively.*

BERNARD *and* JOELLE *finally arrive.*

JEAN-FRANÇOIS Well, you two, it's about time!

JOELLE My car broke down, that's all. Don't carry on so!

_____

[1. To which the English subtitles add: "Funny . . . you don't *look* Jewish!"]

BERNARD Luckily, I was the last one to leave Nice. If I hadn't been, Joelle would be there yet!

JOELLE *finds* LILIANE *to ask her about the particulars of the forthcoming shot.*

LILIANE (*staring at* JOELLE's *striped blouse*) The continuity's off. You weren't wearing that when we left this morning!

Luckily, FERRAND *has given the signal to begin shooting, or* JOELLE *would have had a lot of explaining to do.*

The stuntman drives the blue convertible off camera. He then rehearses coming around the hairpin curve a couple of times, letting the automobile skid perilously close to the road edge. FERRAND *seems satisfied, and the actual shooting begins.*

One camera, placed in the middle of the road, will film the skidding of the car. A second camera, halfway down the ravine, is to film the fall of the automobile as it goes hurtling into space over the road edge. The stuntman's task is to drive the car as fast as possible, turning and skidding on the hairpin curve, abandoning the wheel (without being seen by the first camera, of course) at the very moment the car goes flying down into the ravine.

As often happens in filmmaking, the shooting of this scene (which appeared to be so difficult on paper) goes off without a hitch. Luckily, only one take is needed. JEAN-FRANÇOIS' *blue convertible lies, completely smashed, two hundred feet below.* [FERRAND *rushes over to where the stuntman lies on the ground to make certain he is all right. Then, calling out to the two camera operators to assure himself that everything functioned as planned, he thanks the young man and tells him he is free to leave.*[1]]

JEAN-FRANÇOIS *and* JOELLE *are quite taken aback to see* LILIANE

[1. FERRAND's concern over the stuntman *first,* and the effectiveness of the shot *afterward,* says a lot for his humanity. To judge from the testimony of such action-film stars as Errol Flynn and such cameramen as Hal Mohr, this was not usually the case with Hollywood directors. Some directors (like Michael Curtiz) thought nothing of subjecting stuntmen, extras, and animals to injury and possible death in the interest of getting an arresting shot. The original French script did not stress this point; yet it seemed interesting enough to do so here.]

*suddenly hop into the front seat of the stuntman's personal car
just before he speeds off.*

JEAN-FRANÇOIS   Well, that's something! He was supposed to drive
me back to the studio . . . and there he goes off with Liliane
instead! *Tranquillos!* [let's keep calm!]

Victorine Studios. Exterior. Day.

Arriving in her [little red sports] car, JULIE *notices the stuntman and* LILIANE *piling suitcases into the trunk of an automobile. She parks in front of them and gets out.* JULIE *asks the
stuntman how the shooting went and he tells her it needed
only one take.*

JULIE   (*in English*) Terrific; (*turning to* LILIANE, *in French*)
What are you two doing with all those suitcases?

LILIANE   I might as well tell you right away. I'm in love with him,
and he loves me, too. I'm going to London with him.

JULIE   But the film! It's not finished!

LILIANE   Oh, they can easily get along without me. I'm next to
nothing there.

JULIE   But a person just doesn't walk out on a film in the middle
of shooting![1]

LILIANE   Yes, I suppose so—but I'm not really part of the crew.
I was taken on only in order to please Alphonse.

JULIE   What does Alphonse think about all this?

LILIANE   Tonight he'll get a little surprise!

JULIE   But it'll put him in a horrible state!

LILIANE   He's always in a horrible state! He's a moody child, completely spoiled, and he'll never be a man.

[1. And yet that's exactly what we were told earlier JULIE herself did
two years before.]

JULIE But he loves you! You two were supposed to be married!

LILIANE He's the one who went around telling everybody that. I never mentioned marriage. Just the word is enough to make me want to puke! No, what Alphonse needs is a combination wife, mistress, wet nurse, and little sister. I'm not capable of playing all those roles, even if I wanted to.

JULIE It's very wrong, what you're doing. Don't you realize that? You're being too hard on him!

LILIANE It's all over, anyway. I don't want to hear any more about "poor" Alphonse. Just because a person has had an unhappy childhood doesn't mean he has the right to make everybody else suffer!

Understanding by now that her efforts are useless, JULIE *gets back into her car and drives off onto the lot.*

VICTORINE. SET: THE PARENTS' VILLA. EXTERIOR. DAY.

JULIE *is surprised to see most of the crew standing on the stone steps before the villa. Someone calls out to her:* PIERROT *is taking a souvenir photograph for* SÉVERINE, *who has just finished her last day of shooting.*[1]

Even STACEY *has arrived to take part in the group photo. Her large stomach swelling out under her dress stimulates all sorts of pleasantries.*

BERTRAND Come over here, Stacey! We're all proud of you! To look at you I've the feeling it's due at any moment!

[1. The continuity of this scene is vaguely unsettling. It quite obviously takes place immediately after the previous two scenes. Yet, one cannot but wonder how the crew got back so quickly from *La Vésubie* to pose for such a photograph—and how this happened to be SÉVERINE's last day (since she did not take part in the auto accident sequence).]

STACEY I thought it must be twins—but the doctor assures me there's only one in there, believe it or not!

SÉVERINE (*laughing*) Stacey has all the luck! Now she'll only get close-ups!

The atmosphere is relaxed, merry even, and PIERROT *has a hard time getting everyone to calm down long enough to take a photograph. At the very moment when he announces he is ready to snap the picture,* ALPHONSE *suddenly stops everything.*

PIERROT Careful, nobody move!

ALPHONSE Wait, you can't take it yet. Someone's missing! Where's Liliane?

Seeing his bewilderment JULIE *at first hesitates, then decides to take him aside to explain the situation.*

JULIE Alphonse, I'd like to talk with you for a minute.

They walk away from the group, who regard them curiously. [The ominous music we heard upon JULIE'S *arrival at the Nice Airport fills the sound track once more. Quick close-ups of* PIERROT, *of* MADAME LAJOIE (*who has been sitting not far from the villa steps, knitting as usual*), *watching* JULIE *speaking to* ALPHONSE.] *The atmosphere is far from merry now.*

When JULIE *and* ALPHONSE *return to the steps,* ALPHONSE *appears to have taken whatever* JULIE *has told him quite calmly.*

ALPHONSE She was right to leave. I understand her perfectly. It had to end like this. . . .

Everyone begins posing once more. But now it's SÉVERINE *who interrupts.*

SÉVERINE No, it's not possible! Now Alphonse has run off! Odile! Where's Odile?

And while some of the crew leave to hunt for ALPHONSE, JOELLE *comes over to* JULIE.

JOELLE What's all this about? Tell me!

JULIE Well, Liliane has run off . . . with the English stuntman.

JOELLE And Alphonse knows?

JULIE Yes. I was forced to tell him.

JOELLE With the stuntman yet! As for me, I might leave a guy for a film—but I'd never leave a film for a guy!

In the foreground, Alexandra Stewart, Jacqueline Bisset, Jean-Pierre Léaud.
"Alphonse, I'd like to talk with you for a minute . . ."

Hotel Atlantic. Interior. Night.

We are in FERRAND's *room. He is sleeping restlessly. Over his face are superimposed the colorful illuminated façades of various movie houses.*

In FERRAND's *dreams, the little boy with the long cane walks once more. This time the shot is prolonged enough for us to make out what the iron grille we saw earlier is: the closed front of a movie theater, locked for the night.*

By stretching out his long cane the little boy is at last able to pull toward the iron grille a movable display stand covered with stills from the film currently playing: Orson Welles' Citizen Kane.

With his cane the little boy knocks down all the stills. They fall to the ground immediately on the other side of the grille, close enough for the little boy to reach through and grab them. He gathers them into a pile. [The camera lingers for a moment on a still of Charles Foster Kane as a child of eight (Buddy Swann) struggling with Mister Thatcher (George Coulouris), the famous "Rosebud" sled in the foreground.]

Then, with the pile of stills under one arm, the little boy takes off, racing up the deserted street.

[The scene, although not in color but printed on color stock, nevertheless has a bluish monochromatic cast not evident in the two earlier dream sequences.]

[Cut, once more, to brightly colored shot of entrance to Victorine Studios, shining in the morning sunlight, palm trees rustling.]

In FERRAND's dreams, the little boy with the cane has returned.
"Citizen Kane . . . *the film of films! Probably the one film that has
stimulated more careers in movie-making than any other.*"
—François Truffaut.

VICTORINE STUDIOS. EXTERIOR. DAY.

The following day. Shooting continues despite the absence of ALPHONSE, *who remains shut up in his hotel room.*

Facing the parents' villa set an elevated platform has been erected, on a level with the second story of the villa. Upon this staging stands a window flanked by two wall panels. A camera placed at the farthest end of the platform can therefore film at one and the same time JULIE-PAMELA *drawing back the curtains of her bedroom window and, facing her across empty space,* SÉVERINE *and* ALEXANDRE *standing at a balcony window of their own villa.[1] This camera angle allows the viewer to believe in the topography required by the script: two houses situated facing each other across an expanse of garden.*

JULIE *climbs [barefoot] the tall ladder leading up to the skeleton staging. [The height itself would be more than enough to give many another actress vertigo. Yet* JULIE, *with a determined air that once again reveals the inner strength beneath her seeming fragility, refuses to let the ladder's dangerous wobbling deter her. In the background as she climbs higher and higher we see the white housefronts of suburban Nice, palm trees, and, beyond, the Maritime Alps. The scaffolding, viewed from this angle, looks particularly bizarre, a window frame standing there in the middle of empty space.]*

FERRAND, *who is already up on the scaffold with his cameraman, helps* JULIE *off the ladder. He explains to her that since* AL-PHONSE *is absent the scene will have to be changed.* JULIE *must stand alone at the window; then, while calling across to*

[1. Yet, we had already been told that *yesterday* was SÉVERINE's last day of shooting—hence, the taking of the group photograph. One has the feeling that the continuity was rearranged in the cutting room for dramatic purposes, and this script changed accordingly.]

SÉVERINE *and* ALEXANDRE, *she can turn to face the camera behind her, as if she were talking to* ALPHONSE *still in bed.* FERRAND *himself will answer her,* [ALPHONSE's *own lines being "looped in" later*].

WALTER, *overhearing* FERRAND, *can not refrain from a bit of kidding.*

WALTER Oh, that Alphonse, always in love, always in a stew!

FERRAND Someday I am going to make a film called *The Stews of Love!* . . . Good, let's go![1]

Shooting begins. We watch the sequence with JULIE, SÉVERINE, *and* ALEXANDRE *being shot twice in succession.*

In the cutting room FERRAND *and his two editors are viewing the location footage shot at La Vésubie. We watch the scene unfold upon the tiny editing machine screen in various manners: the blue convertible goes hurtling down into the gorge; then, suddenly, it comes flying back up through the air and lands on the road, moving backward around the hairpin curve. We see it first from the point of view of the camera that had been set up in the middle of the road, then from the point of view of the camera halfway down the gorge. Finally,* FERRAND *indicates the exact moment when the scene should be cut in order to conceal the sight of the stuntman jumping from the car.* [FERRAND's *fingers, making a scissorlike movement before the flickering image on the Moritone, look like those of a child playing at creating silhouettes upon a wall.*]

HOTEL ATLANTIC. INTERIOR. NIGHT.

JOELLE *walks along an upstairs corridor. She stops before a door. The key is in the lock; so she opens it. To her surprise*

[1. In French here there is a pun on the word *salade* which can mean not only "salad" but also "mess-up." FERRAND states he is one day going to make a film called *Les Salades de l'Amour.*]

she finds BERNARD *and* ODILE *in bed together.* BERNARD, *crimson with confusion, ducks under the covers.*

JOELLE *shuts the door, smiling to herself.* [*She puts on her glasses to verify the door number.*] *Yes, she had made a mistake. It's the next door she wants.*

JOELLE (*knocking loudly*) Alphonse, I know you're in there! Open up! Everyone is waiting for you downstairs! Everybody's asking for you!

ALPHONSE No! Nobody's asking for me!

JOELLE But they are! Séverine leaves tonight. And then Julie . . .

ALPHONSE I don't want to see anyone! I don't want to see anyone, Joelle! Do you hear me?

JOELLE *shrugs and leaves.*

HOTEL DINING ROOM. INTERIOR. NIGHT.

SÉVERINE *is having her last meal with the other actors:* ALEXANDRE, JULIE, STACEY. JOELLE *has just rejoined them.*[1] *At the moment,* SÉVERINE *is in top form.*

SÉVERINE There was once an actor who all of his life dreamed of playing Hamlet. Finally, when he couldn't get anyone else to finance it, he produced it himself. But he was so awful that every night he was booed. Well, one evening, he'd had enough. So he stopped, right in the middle of the "To be or not to be" soliloquy, and turned to his audience, and shouted: "Don't blame me! I didn't write this shit!"

[1. If this scene follows directly after the one preceding, there is something unsettling in ODILE's absence from SÉVERINE's farewell dinner. The charming young make-up girl had been one of SÉVERINE's closest friends throughout shooting (or so we assumed), and it is hard to believe she would be too busy in bed with BERNARD to pass up this farewell party.]

"A film of fiction which imitates the filmed journal of a shooting . . ."

Everyone roars as SÉVERINE *translates the punch line (which she had first delivered in English) into French.* SÉVERINE, *already in her cups, invites everyone to drink champagne with her. While the waiter sets more bottles on the table,* SÉVERINE *summons over* FERRAND *and* BERTRAND *who have been dining quietly at a nearby table.* FERRAND *and* BERTRAND *comply.* SÉVERINE *now invites* WALTER, WALTER'S *assistants, and the set photographer* PIERROT *to join her table as well.*

SÉVERINE Come on, all you misogynists![1] Come over here and have some champagne!

In her expansiveness, SÉVERINE *even invites a young man sitting alone at a table to join them. He turns out to be one of the hotel's clients: [a tall, shy young man, with a beard, rather intellectual-looking].* JEAN-FRANÇOIS *explains the situation to him; that they are a movie crew and that this is a farewell celebration.*

While all this joyful commotion is going on, JULIE *has remained silent. Suddenly she gets up from her chair, thinking no one will notice her departure amid all the confusion. She goes over to* JOELLE.

JULIE I think somebody should go upstairs and get Alphonse.

JOELLE I've already tried. He's locked himself in. What's more, he'd only spoil all the fun with his moody act.

JULIE You're too hard on him.

JOELLE Hard, hard. . . . It's just that I've had to put up with him longer than you!

JULIE Well then, I'll go and get him myself.

JOELLE Oh, all right, I'll try once more!

As JOELLE *departs to return upstairs,* JULIE *is suddenly called back to the table by* SÉVERINE, *who wants to show her some huge color stills that* PIERROT *has been passing around.*

SÉVERINE Julie! Come here and take a look! These are marvelous! *(pointing to a photo of* JULIE *and turning to the others)* Isn't she lovely! . . . Oh, one of me! . . . Ugh! What a horror!

[1. The subtitler translates this as "all you male chauvinists"—which in these times seems more apt than the original French.]

And, while studying the photographs, SÉVERINE *grows melancholy.*

SÉVERINE   What funny lives we lead! We meet, we work together, we love each other. . . . Well, what of it? We never have the time to take hold of anything before—phfft!—it's no longer there!

Her eyes shining with tears, SÉVERINE *holds out the palm of her empty hand to* JULIE.

SÉVERINE   You see? It's no longer there!

The others are suddenly silent.

STAIRWAY AND HOTEL CORRIDOR. INTERIOR. NIGHT.

We find our cast and crew climbing the stairs to go to bed. ALEXANDRE *is holding forth about his co-star.*

ALEXANDRE   What an extraordinary woman that Séverine is! I remember a film we made in Italy together. She was so brilliant and so outrageous that the director never stopped saying: "Why, she's better than Duse! She's superior to Eleonora Duse!" I ended by nicknaming her: "Duse-and-a-half"![1]

Arriving on the landing, the group stop to make their last goodnights before turning in. JOELLE *comes down the corridor.*

FERRAND   Oh, Joelle! Have you seen Alphonse?

JOELLE   He refuses to come out. He's shut himself up in his room. He won't listen to anyone. . . .

[1. Another untranslatable pun. In French it is a play on the words *Duse-et-demi* ("Duse-and-a-half") and *Douze-et-demi* ("Twelve-and-a-half"), an obvious reference to Fellini's *Huit-et-demi* ("8½"). The English subtitler solved it by making up another, but far less witty, pun: "Me-Dusa."]

FERRAND You've seen him then?

JOELLE No, not even that!

FERRAND All the same, he should realize Séverine is—

His words are interrupted by a strange apparition: ALPHONSE, *in a long nightshirt, who moves like a sleepwalker toward the group.*

ALPHONSE Would someone give me ten thousand francs[1] to go to a whorehouse?

No one answers. Finally, FERRAND *goes over to* ALPHONSE *and gently leads him back to his room, speaking quietly all the while.*

FERRAND Listen to me, Alphonse. You are going back into your room right now, you are going to reread your script, you are going to work on it for a little while, and then you are going to try to get some sleep. Tomorrow is a work day—and work is the important thing. You are a very good actor, Alphonse. Your work is going well. Yes, I realize there also has to be a private life—but private life is messy for everyone. Films are more harmonious than life, Alphonse. There are no traffic jams in films, no dead waits. Films move forward like trains, you understand, like trains in the night. People like us are happy only in our work, you must realize that, in our work of making movies. Good night, Alphonse. I'm counting on you.

FERRAND *closes the door of the room on* ALPHONSE.

JULIE'S HOTEL ROOM. INTERIOR. NIGHT.

A short while later. JULIE *is hard at work, learning her lines and improving her French pronunciation with the aid of a*

[1. Approximately $25.00 in 1972.]

tiny tape recorder. [She seems to have trouble with the word
déguisement *("fancy-dress") and repeats the line in which it
occurs twice.]*

The telephone rings.

JULIE *(not at all pleased by the interruption)* Hello?

ALPHONSE *(voice-off)* Julie? Alphonse. I'm leaving right now,
Julie, but I wanted to tell you first, because you've always
been very honest with me. I haven't told Ferrand. You can
break it to him later.

JULIE Wait, Alphonse! I must speak to you!

*She hangs up the phone, hurriedly throws a white raincoat over
her nightdress, and leaves the room.*

JULIE *walks rapidly down the corridor toward* ALPHONSE's *room.*

*She pushes the door, which is partly open. By the time she
enters,* ALPHONSE *has just about finished packing.*

JULIE Why must you carry on like this, Alphonse? You can't
leave!

ALPHONSE I am leaving, Julie. I'm retiring from all this.

JULIE No, Alphonse, you must stay and finish the film.

ALPHONSE Even if I remained, I couldn't work in the state I'm
in! I'm no longer capable physically! Do you, of all people,
find it normal that someone could just stop loving you from
one hour to another and take off with a complete stranger, just
like that? What it proves is that it was false right from the
start. Everything was rotten even then!

JULIE I know what you're going through, Alphonse. It hurts
terribly. Believe me, I know. But I also know that Liliane loves
you, no matter how it looks right now. Besides, try to see it from
her point of view. You must admit you're a bit—egotistical.
You know how difficult it is to live with any actor, especially
for someone not in the business like Liliane.

ALPHONSE I agree. But that's still no reason for her to take off
with the first comer—some shitty English stuntman!

JULIE *(smiling)* Now wait a minute, I'm English, too! As a
matter of fact, I do know all about these stuntmen. You don't
need much of an imagination to guess what will happen. At

first, he'll take Liliane everywhere in his work with him. Then he'll grow tired of that, and she'll feel herself lost, all alone in London. I'll wager that in two weeks' time she'll be back.

ALPHONSE You really think so?

JULIE Yes.

ALPHONSE Even if she does return, it's all over. No more of that for me, thank you! I prefer to suffer. Do you know something, Julie? I've discovered something truly frightening: that one can love, be in love to the point of dying, with somebody one despises, somebody whose every gesture, whose every word, whose every thought one detests!

JULIE Oh, no, Alphonse, don't say that! Who are you to despise another human being like that? Even if you believe now that you made a mistake, you should never be ashamed of having loved someone. When you speak of Liliane with such contempt, it's as if you . . . degraded yourself. . . .

ALPHONSE Perhaps you're right, Julie. Anyway, even before Liliane, all my love affairs have ended catastrophically. I've believed for too long now that women were magical creatures.

JULIE Of course, they're not magical creatures—or, rather, men are magical also. Everyone is magical—or no one is magical!

ALPHONSE Then, too, you know I'm certain Ferrand is completely wrong: life is more important than making movies. That's why I have to leave. Thanks, Julie. Thanks for everything.

ALPHONSE *closes the zipper on his last valise.*

JULIE You musn't act like a fool, Alphonse. You must remain here and finish your work.

She takes a step toward him.

Night. All the corridors and stairways of the hotel are vacant. [Various shots of silent corridors, empty stairways.]

Down in the hotel lobby, the night clerk snores on a couch. ODILE *comes by to awaken him.*

ODILE Hey, Lucien—is your clock working?

Jacqueline Bisset and Jean-Pierre Léaud.

LUCIEN (*only half awake*) Yes, yes, yes . . .

ODILE But it's six o'clock! Time to make coffee for your customers!

We next see ODILE *standing before* JULIE's *room. She knocks. No answer. She opens the door. The room is empty, the bed has not been slept in.*

Hastening down the corridor once more, ODILE *bumps into* JOELLE *who holds an elaborate period gown on a hanger high in the air before her.*

ODILE Oh, Joelle, you haven't seen Julie, have you?

JOELLE Uh uh. Have *you* seen Lajoie anywhere? Do you know what that idiot did? He thought the fancy-dress sequence had already been shot—and so he sent all the costumes back to Paris!

ODILE What? Then you've been up since three?

JOELLE Worse than that! I never got to bed at all! I've been out at the airport all night trying to recover every costume. Otherwise, we'd never be able to shoot today.

ODILE I wonder where I can find Julie.

JOELLE You've looked in her room?

ODILE Yes. She didn't sleep there. The bed's still made.

JOELLE If you want my opinion, everybody connected with this film is definitely nuts!

JOELLE *and* ODILE *disappear together down the stairs.*

We are in ALPHONSE's *room.* JULIE *lies asleep in bed next to him. She wakes up, looks around confusedly. Then she gets up, quietly walking around the bed in order to reset the alarm clock on the night table. She must have made some sound, for* ALPHONSE *suddenly sits up.*

ALPHONSE What time is it?

JULIE (*very tenderly*) Six o'clock.

ALPHONSE Why are you leaving?

JULIE I've got to go to work. You can sleep for two more hours. I've set the alarm for eight.

Jacqueline Bisset and Jean-Pierre Léaud.

ALPHONSE Stay with me.

JULIE I can't.

ALPHONSE Please!

JULIE I have an early make-up call. And I also have to have my hair set for the fancy-dress sequence.

ALPHONSE Wait, please wait! Kiss me. (*they kiss*) You won't forget, will you? We'll leave together on the last day of shooting, just the two of us. We'll go somewhere—anywhere!

JULIE Sleep!

JULIE is very maternal with ALPHONSE. She treats him more like a sick child than like a lover. After one final kiss, she leaves.

JULIE opens the door carefully to make certain the corridor is empty. [At the far end of the hall the sky is a brilliant blue already beyond the windows. JULIE runs toward her own room, her white raincoat flying out behind her.]

Down in the lobby ODILE still anxiously waits for JULIE. But here she comes now! The two young women kiss warmly, then rush out of the hotel together. A municipal truck passes, sprinkling the street clean.

The alarm on ALPHONSE's night table now shows eight o'clock. ALPHONSE is wide awake. He sits up in bed, telephoning.

ALPHONSE Hello? Doctor Nelson? This is Alphonse. . . . I've something to tell you. I'm in love with your wife. I've gone to bed with her. Set her free!

He hangs up.

VICTORINE STUDIOS. INTERIOR. DAY.

We hear a voice over a loudspeaker: "JULIE BAKER is wanted on the set . . . JULIE BAKER on the set, please!"

Jean-Pierre Léaud.
"Hello? Doctor Nelson? . . . I'm in love with your wife. I've gone to bed with her. Set her free!"

Dressed in the beautiful black and white period gown she is to wear in the fancy-dress sequence, JULIE *is about to leave her dressing room. The sound of the telephone ringing stops her.* ODILE *has answered. She sets the receiver down and runs over to the door.*

ODILE   Julie! Julie! I think it's your husband.

JULIE returns, picks up the receiver. After a moment, she asks ODILE *to leave her alone, making a gesture for her to shut the door behind her.*

In the studio administration office BERNARD *is trying to be reimbursed for a bill for prop expenses.*

LAJOIE   Not now! I haven't time for that now!

BERNARD   I know! And when I come around later you'll tell me it's too late!

He leaves, swearing loudly. LAJOIE, *who all the while has been on the phone, shouts into the receiver.*

LAJOIE   You've looked everywhere? You're sure he's not in his hotel room?

He hangs up. He turns around to look at ALEXANDRE, *who has been sitting in a chair listening intently.*

LAJOIE   Alphonse has taken off!

ALEXANDRE   Shit!

BERTRAND   [*who has been rushing about the office*] Do you think he might have returned to Paris?

ALEXANDRE   [*who knows all about flight schedules, thanks to* CHRISTIAN] There's a plane at 8:50 and another at 10:10.

BERTRAND   Lajoie, call the airport!

JEAN-FRANÇOIS   [*who has also overheard most of the conversation*] While you're doing that, I'm off to the airport. If he's there, I'll bring him back if I have to bind and gag him!

At the same moment JEAN-FRANÇOIS *is rushing out,* JOELLE *bursts in.*

JOELLE   Well, kiddies, we're really up shit creek now!

JEAN-FRANÇOIS We already know. Alphonse has disappeared. I'm off to find him.

JOELLE Alphonse? I'm talking about Julie! I don't know what happened, a fit of hysteria or what—but, anyway, she's locked herself in her dressing room. She won't talk to anybody, not even Odile. You can hear her crying behind the door.

JEAN-FRANÇOIS *takes off, not wanting to hear any more bad news.*

Standing before the closed door of JULIE's *dressing room are* ALEXANDRE, BERTRAND, JOELLE. *Even the young production secretary,* CAROLINE, *has joined them in their vigil.* ODILE, *who has never left her post, explains the situation to the others.*

ODILE First, she got a telephone call. From Doctor Nelson, I think. Then she asked me to leave. That's when she locked herself in.

JOELLE (*knocking on the door*) Julie, it's me! Open the door!

ALEXANDRE Julie, please open up. We're your friends.

BERTRAND It's me, Bertrand. Your producer! I want to help you, Julie.

The door remains shut.

JOELLE (*in a low whisper*) Keep quiet, all of you! You don't think she's doing something silly in there . . . ?

STACEY, *who has just heard the news, arrives,* [*plodding up the stairs. It is obviously a difficult job in her condition.*]

STACEY Have you succeeded in talking to her yet?

BERTRAND No. She's locked herself in. She refuses to open the door.

STACEY *knocks lightly on the door. She speaks in English:* "It's Stacey, Julie! Please let me in!"[1] *To the great surprise of the*

[1. Alexandra Stewart, who plays STACEY, speaks English as perfectly as she speaks French. This lovely Canadian-born actress has made the greater part of her career in France, but has also appeared in such American films as Otto Preminger's Exodus (1960) and Arthur Penn's Mickey One (1965).]

In front of Julie's dressing room door, Nike Arrighi, Jean-Pierre Aumont, Jean Champion, Nathalie Baye, and Caroline, the production secretary.

others, the key turns in the lock. The door opens—but only wide enough to allow STACEY *to enter. Then it closes once more.*

BERTRAND   Now that takes the cake! She refuses to let us in, but she opens up for Stacey!

ALEXANDRE *(smiling)* Perhaps she thinks an expectant mother will understand her problem better?

LAJOIE, *this time escorted by his dour wife, arrives all out of breath on the landing.*

LAJOIE   Monsieur Bertrand, we've searched everywhere for Alphonse: the airport, the hotel—he can't be found!

JOELLE   Suddenly it all makes sense. First, Julie didn't sleep in her room last night. Then Doctor Nelson telephoned Julie this morning long-distance. Now Alphonse has taken off. I don't have to draw you all a diagram, do I?

This last question sets off a violent tirade on the part of MADAME LAJOIE, *whom everyone considered almost a mute, since she has never yet uttered one word since the start of shooting to anyone other than her husband.*

MADAME LAJOIE [*coming up the stairs, her face more and more contorted with rage*] What kind of a world is this, your precious cinema? What kind of a world is this where everybody is on such intimate terms with everybody else, where everybody lies—where everybody sleeps with everybody else! Do you find all that normal? . . . Your precious cinema! To me it's rotten, it stinks to high heaven! I *despise* your cinema. . . . Yes, I despise it! [*she raises her fist before her face, screaming hysterically*]

BERTRAND *(to* LAJOIE*)* Listen, old man, that's enough from your wife. Take her out of here and for God's sake calm her down!

The group separate.

BERTRAND *and* ALEXANDRE *reenter the administration office, still discussing what has just happened.*

ALEXANDRE   No, I think that poor woman is wrong. Oh, it may be that in our world things are a bit more obvious, out in the open more—but love leads everybody by the nose everywhere, and not just here!

They have hardly entered, when STACEY *appears, all out of breath.*

BERTRAND You've talked to Julie?

STACEY Yes. She has a craving for tub butter. You know, the kind that's sold in huge chunks.

BERTRAND (*dumbfounded*) Tub butter?

STACEY Yes. We must absolutely find some for her. Surely one of you must know where to get country butter around here!

BERTRAND But what's come over her? Has she gone completely off her rocker? What did she say to you? What's she doing?

STACEY She's crying—she's crying. She'll stop finally. But right now we must get her some tub butter.

BERTRAND (*to* BERNARD, *who has been rummaging around inside the inner office*) Did you hear that, Bernard? You'll have to hunt up some tub butter!

STACEY Yes, Bernard, you must—at once!

BERNARD Oh, no, you don't! I'm in charge of props—and there's no tub butter mentioned in the script! That's not in my contract!

BERTRAND Now, Bernard, that's not like you! After all, we movie people are one big family!

ALEXANDRE Ah, yes! But the House of Atreus was one big family, too![1]

BERTRAND Well then, I'll go and dig up some tub butter myself!

And BERTRAND *leaves, soon followed by* STACEY *and* BERNARD. ALEXANDRE, *still smiling, is left alone with* CAROLINE, *the pro-*

[1. Atreus was the father of Agamemnon and Menelaus, upon whose house his brother Thyestes pronounced a curse. The various ways in which this curse is worked out is the subject of many Greek tragedies, including Aeschylus' trilogy, the *Oresteia*, and both Euripides' and Sophocles' versions of the *Electra* legend. The English subtitler rewrites ALEXANDRE's line as: "Ah, yes, but so were the families in Greek tragedies!"]

duction secretary. He wanders into her outer office and sits down on the edge of her desk.

ALEXANDRE   All the same, Bertrand's lucky that Julie's whim is so inexpensive! Believe me, I've known far more costly ones in my day! There was once an Austrian actress, I remember, who was one of Hollywood's all-time glamour queens. Well, she missed the wet climate of her native Tyrol so much that do you know what she finally had installed in the garden of her California estate? A rain machine! So, you see, Caroline, tub butter, by comparison . . . ![1] (*he shrugs philosophically*)

Walking past the studio washrooms. JOELLE *gets the surprise of her life when* BERTRAND *calls out to her to come in. He is standing before one of the sinks, kneading sticks of butter. On the shelf above the sink is a small mountain of sticks, each still wrapped in its foil.*

BERTRAND   Ah, Joelle, you came by at just the right time! Would you help me with this mess?

JOELLE   But that's not tub butter!

BERTRAND   You don't say! It seems there's no such thing any more in the entire *Alpes-Maritimes* region! So I got an idea: why not take a lot of sticks, unwrap them, mash them together—and after it's all done up in gauze who's to know the difference?

JOELLE   Do you think it'll work? I wonder!

BERTRAND   It had better work! All the same, what a crazy racket we're in!

The two set to work.

---

1. This story of the rain machine, possibly apocryphal, has been told about quite a few "transplanted" European movie queens, including Luise Rainer and Hedy Lamarr.

Administration office. Interior. Day.

The telephone rings. CAROLINE, *who is typing now that* ALEXANDRE *has left, picks up the receiver.*

CAROLINE Hello!

Karting de la Siesta. Exterior. Day.

[*The Karting de la Siesta is a miniature auto racetrack in Antibes, less than ten miles away from the Victorine. Karting is a sport very popular on the Riviera, in which a driver steers a miniature racing car (a "go-kart" in U.S. parlance) completely lacking an outside body, springs, or even a transmission.*]

JEAN-FRANÇOIS *is calling from a phone booth.*

JEAN-FRANÇOIS I've found our Alphonse. But if I tell you where, you won't believe me. Anyway, I'm bringing him back pronto!

JEAN-FRANÇOIS *hangs up, then leaps over a pile of automobile tires which serve as the walls of the track. He stands in the middle of the raceway and stops one of the cars. The driver is* ALPHONSE, *of course,* [*a blue crash helmet on his head.* ALPHONSE *glares up at* JEAN-FRANÇOIS.]

Studio washroom. Interior. Day.

FERRAND *suddenly comes upon* BERTRAND *and* JOELLE.

FERRAND   So here you are! I've been looking everywhere!

BERTRAND   We're manufacturing tub butter for Julie. How is she?

FERRAND   She seems fine.

BERTRAND *proudly holds up the dome-shaped mound of butter, wrapped in gauze and sitting on a plate.*

BERTRAND (*handing the plate to* JOELLE) I made it. But I'll be damned if I'll bring it to her.

JOELLE   Me, neither! I'm like the old cook in *The Rules of the Game:* "I accept diets, but I don't allow fads!"[1]

And JOELLE *in turn passes the plate—to* FERRAND.

FERRAND   O.K. Agreed!

FERRAND, *carrying the plate of "tub butter," knocks on* JULIE's *dressing room door. A muffled voice bids him enter.*

JULIE *is seated on a couch at the far end of the room. [The dressing room appears changed from our earlier view of it, before* JULIE *had arrived from America. Now there is a huge color photo of* DOCTOR NELSON *on one wall. A white-and-gold miniature tapestry signed by Jean Cocteau also hangs below and to one side of* DOCTOR NELSON's *picture.]*

FERRAND   Well, Julie—here's what you asked for.

JULIE   Oh, I couldn't have!

[1. In Jean Renoir's *La Règle du Jeu* (1939) one of the eccentric guests at the château demands that only sea salt be used in her food— and then sprinkled on only *after* cooking. When this information is conveyed to the head cook, he explodes.]

FERRAND *sets the plate down on a table and goes to sit beside her on the couch.*

JULIE Forgive me. I'm so ashamed. (*she begins to cry once more*) I'll be all right if you just leave me alone for a minute. I realize I'm not acting like a professional. Believe me, I don't like being this way. Everyone is sitting around waiting—and all because of me! I've never done this before. . . .

FERRAND It's not serious, Julie. We can wait a little longer, you know. I'm going to talk to Jean-François. We can always change the shooting schedule.

JULIE Oh, no, you mustn't do that because of me! I—I'll be myself in a minute. Just give me a bit more time. Could you lend me your handkerchief?

FERRAND Yes. Of course.

JULIE *takes* FERRAND's *handkerchief and dries her tears.*

JULIE Thank you. I must look a fright. (*she suddenly starts sobbing again*) But Alphonse . . . why did Alphonse do it? He understood nothing!

FERRAND Alphonse is a child, Julie. He acted like a child. You know, Julie, I don't know your husband very well, but I've nevertheless seen enough of him to realize that he's an extraordinary man. So then . . .

JULIE Yes, he is an extraordinary man. You don't know how much so! When I had my—nervous breakdown, he did something very serious: he left his wife and children—he abandoned his family for me. He gave up the life he had so carefully constructed for over twenty years. He did all that for me—devoting his whole life to me! He tried to make me into a responsible woman. Right now he must be thinking how it's all been a horrible waste! (*she cries*)

FERRAND [*gently pushing back a strand of* JULIE's *hair that has fallen down over her cheek*]: I don't believe that, Julie. When your husband finds out exactly what happened, he will understand. He'll forget. Everything will be the same as before, I'm certain of it.

JULIE Do you think so? Even if what you say is true, I won't ever be able to forget. It's entirely thanks to him and all he has

taught me that I now feel myself strong enough to change my
life. I've made up my mind. I'm going to live alone. I've had
enough of disguises, of all these silly masquerades. I'm going
to retire from films. I realize now that life is disgusting!

SET: SÉVERINE'S DINING ROOM. INTERIOR. DAY.

In order that the work day will not be completely wasted,
JEAN-FRANÇOIS *has assembled the crew to record "wild tracks"*
(i.e., various sounds that can be mixed in with the dialogue
and music later on whenever certain background noises are
needed).

JEAN-FRANÇOIS Are we all here? Since we can't shoot as planned,
let's do some wild tracks for the fancy-dress sequence.

SOUND ENGINEER I need applause first. O.K. Go ahead.

The electricians on the catwalks high above the set applaud
along with the various grips and technicians below. ODILE *and*
JOELLE *also join in.*

SOUND ENGINEER That's enough applause! What I need now are
murmurs. But, for God's sake, when you talk, don't talk about
movies!

Everyone complies.

SOUND ENGINEER Thanks. Now some more applause, please.

Suddenly, everyone stops applauding, even though the sound-
man has given them no such instructions. DOCTOR NELSON *has*
appeared on the set, escorted by STACEY. *The crew makes a*
path to let them pass.

STACEY *informs the doctor that* JULIE's *dressing room is just*
up the stairs and at the end of the corridor. The doctor leaves.
The moment he is gone everyone rushes over to STACEY.

JEAN-FRANÇOIS What's up with Nelson here?

STACEY Well, nobody seemed to be doing anything—so I took

the bull by the horns and called him. He agreed to come right away. And so here he is![1]

JOELLE Terrific!

JULIE'S DRESSING ROOM. INTERIOR. DAY.

DOCTOR NELSON *opens the door. He sees* JULIE. *He looks into her eyes, and smiles.*

NELSON Julie . . .

SÉVERINE'S DINING ROOM. INTERIOR. DAY.

The normal activity preceding shooting has resumed. On the catwalks above the set the electricians are arranging various lights. ODILE *is combing* ALPHONSE'S *hair.* ALPHONSE *is now dressed in an elegant period costume [that lends him a certain Byronic air. For all that, his face betrays confusion]. He calls* JOELLE *over.*

[1. A few details here which seem bothersome, although perhaps this is nit-picking. First, although STACEY speaks perfect English, she gives DOCTOR NELSON the directions to JULIE's dressing room in French. It would have been more logical for her to give them in English. Next, until now, one had somehow assumed that the dressing rooms were located in a building separate from the soundstages, and therefore STACEY and NELSON would not have had to cross this set at all. Finally, we were not told *where* NELSON was when he received ALPHONSE's telephone call. This viewer somehow assumed he had returned to the States. Now, since he got back to Nice so swiftly, he must have been either in Paris or London.]

Nathalie Baye, Nike Arrighi, Jean-Pierre Léaud.
"Yes, it's a fine idea: to quit making movies!"

ALPHONSE Joelle, I'm a real shit. I fucked it up royally this time! I was going over to see Julie right now but I honestly didn't know what to say to her. Do you think I should apologize?

JOELLE Listen to me, Alphonse, and listen to me good this time! The less you say, the better!

After imparting such laconic advice, JOELLE *is ready to get back to her duties, but* ALPHONSE *restrains her.*

ALPHONSE Joelle?

JOELLE What is it now?

ALPHONSE You know, I've been thinking a lot lately. I've decided to quit making movies!

JOELLE (*laughing*) That's a very good idea. Yes, it's a fine idea: to quit making movies!

She dashes off. [ALPHONSE *appears highly disconcerted. Obviously that was not the response he had expected.*]

FERRAND *calls over* ODILE, *who has finally finished combing* ALPHONSE's *hair.*

FERRAND Odile, are you going up to Julie's dressing room now?

ODILE Yes.

He hands ODILE *a sheet of paper upon which he has just finished scribbling something.*

FERRAND Good. Then give her this. Tell her it's the new dialogue for the scene. She's to learn it right away.

ODILE Yes, sir.

In JULIE's *dressing room,* DOCTOR NELSON *holds out a pill and a glass of water.*

NELSON (*in English*) Julie, now you must take this.

JULIE (*in English*) I've got to work. You don't think it'll slow me down, do you?

NELSON (*in English*) No. It'll just calm you a bit, that's all. Come on! (*Julie swallows the pill*) Good!

They face each other, smiling. ODILE *enters.*

ODILE Julie, can I make you up now?

[DOCTOR NELSON *leaves as the two young women chat.*]

Jacqueline Bisset, Jean-Pierre Léaud, François Truffaut. Personal problems
no longer matter . . .

JULIE Yes, yes, Odile. Oh, I'm so very happy, Odile! (*kissing* ODILE *impulsively*) Now let's make ourselves beautiful!

JULIE *sits down at her make-up table.* ODILE *hands her the text* FERRAND *has given her.*

ODILE Monsieur Ferrand gave me this for you. It's some new dialogue for the scene.

JULIE *places the sheet against the mirror.*

JULIE (*reading aloud*) "Even if what you say is true, I won't ever be able to forget. I've made up my mind. I'm going to live alone. I realize now that life is disgusting."

JULIE *stares into her own mirrored face.*

JULIE Well, that one never loses *his* bearings![1]

The set of SÉVERINE's *dining room has been modified in order for it to be used for the fancy-dress sequence. Huge blue velvet draperies cover the walls. Many lighted candles, arranged vertically to form stylized chandeliers, seem to be the sole light source in the room.*

Shooting is about to begin. After all that has occurred, the crew seems especially silent and tense. FERRAND *is standing talking to* WALTER *and another technician.[2] He gives the starting signal in an unaccustomed whisper.*

FERRAND Do you feel ready, Julie?

JULIE Yes.

FERRAND Then let's begin. (*quietly*) Camera . . . .

JULIE *stands before one of the swirling blue draperies. [She is dressed in the lovely black and white period gown we saw her wearing for the first time when she received* DOCTOR NELSON's *telephone call (and which we saw even before that when* JOELLE *carried it on a hanger down the hotel corridor*

[1. The English subtitle rephrases it: "That man has a one-track mind!"]

[2. Another example here in the actual film of Truffaut's throwaway brilliance. As FERRAND and the technicians talk, we see directly between them an empty canvas-back chair with the name ALEXANDRE on it. Only later in the scene will the full implication of this shot be evident.]

. . . cinema rules the day.

while she spoke to ODILE). *In her right hand* JULIE *holds the trick candle that* BERNARD *had been so proud of "inventing" the first day of shooting.*]

JULIE-PAMELA   "I've made up my mind. I'm going to live alone. I realize now that life is disgusting."

ALPHONSE *comes over to her.*

ALPHONSE   "No. Life is not disgusting."

FERRAND *gives a signal to the sound engineer, who starts the music of the playback.* [*It is the theme we heard earlier over the phone in the administration office: slow, haunting, lushly romantic.*]

JULIE *and* ALPHONSE *cross the set to the cadence of the music and sit down alongside each other on a small settee.* ALPHONSE *tenderly caresses* JULIE'S *cheek.*

The take ends. [*In the film version, one is especially moved by the rapt look on* ODILE'S *face, who follows* JULIE'S *movements during the take with a mixture of admiration and love.*] JULIE *asks* WALTER *if she held the trick candle correctly. The director of photography assures her it worked perfectly.*

ALPHONSE *turns and explains to* JULIE *that he is going to stroke her cheek with his other hand during the next take in order not to cover her face before the camera. Personal problems no longer count: cinema rules the day once more . . . .*

Another version of the same shot. While the camera tracks, JULIE *and* ALPHONSE, *still to the cadence of the playback, cross the set.*

Suddenly, BERTRAND *arrives in a state of great agitation. He wants to see* FERRAND *immediately, but* JEAN-FRANÇOIS *manages to stop him.* BERTRAND *breaks away. Finally,* JOELLE *succeeds in restraining the producer until the long take is over.*

When FERRAND *says he is satisfied with the shot,* JOELLE *frees* BERTRAND.

BERTRAND (*in a toneless voice, to the entire crew*):   Alexandre is dead. He was returning from the airport where he'd gone to pick up Christian. A truck smashed into their car. Christian is

seriously hurt, but he'll pull through. Alexandre died on the
way to the hospital.[1]

VICTORINE STUDIOS. PARISIAN SQUARE SET.
EXTERIOR. DAY.

FERRAND, *at the wheel of an automobile, drives round and
round the Parisian square. It has rained earlier, and the car
splashes water all over the empty sidewalks as it races past.
[The entire scene is viewed in one held long shot. If we did
not hear* FERRAND's *voice-over, we would not even know it was
he driving the automobile.]*

FERRAND (*voice-over*) This morning Alexandre was buried in a
little cemetery on the heights of Nice. We are now awaiting
the arrival of the representative from the British insurance
company. With him rests the fate of our film. Ever since I
first began making movies I have always feared what has finally
happened: the death of an actor in the middle of shooting.
Along with Alexandre, a whole era of moviemaking is fast
disappearing. Films will soon be shot in the streets—without
stars, without scripts. A production like *Meet Pamela* will soon
be obsolete.

[1. The manner of ALEXANDRE's death is similar to that of Truffaut's
good friend and star of *Soft Skin*, Françoise Dorléac. Mlle. Dorléac,
sister of Catherine Deneuve, was rushing to the Nice Airport on June
26, 1967, to catch a plane back to Paris, when her car overturned to
avoid hitting a truck. The twenty-five-year-old actress, whose career
was leading her to international stardom, burned to death in the
upturned auto.]

Screening room. Interior. Day.

Upon the screen within the screen we watch the last sequence
ALEXANDRE *shot: the scene where he and* SÉVERINE *wave to*
JULIE *standing at the window of her bedroom and invite her*
and ALPHONSE *to come over and share breakfast with them.*
SÉVERINE *and* ALEXANDRE *are both merry.* JULIE-PAMELA *opens*
the false window and calls out to them. At the end of the take,
even as we hear FERRAND'S *voice on the sound track call out,*
"Cut!", we see ALEXANDRE, *as a joke, begin to climb over the*
balcony.

ALEXANDRE (*to* JULIE) Wait for me! I'm coming to join you!

SÉVERINE *lets out a frightened yell as* ALEXANDRE *almost loses*
his balance on the balustrade. She pulls him back onto the
balcony and they embrace, laughing.

The lights come up in the screening room.

Present are FERRAND, JOELLE, BERTRAND, *the representative of*
the English insurance company; plus a French insurance
broker who serves as translator.

[*There is a long moment of silence.* ALEXANDRE *still seems so*
alive. Finally, BERTRAND *speaks.*]

BERTRAND In some odd way I'd been expecting this accident. It
was for that reason I insisted on giving Alexandre a chauffeur.
The man never felt comfortable in any one place, he was always
rushing off to somewhere else. Alexandre was a man on the run!

As he speaks, BERTRAND *has gotten up. He and* FERRAND *walk*
along the side of the room toward the screen.

FERRAND I don't agree. Alexandre felt at home everywhere. He
loved to talk with everybody. He lived in the present. Remember
how he never seemed able to leave a place? And it's for that

very reason he died . . . because he was late, and he didn't want to keep us waiting. In truth, one could say that Alexandre is dead out of generosity for us.

BERTRAND Well, maybe so. . . .

FERRAND *and* BERTRAND *have retraced their steps. They are now facing the two insurance men who have also gotten out of their chairs by now.*

BERTRAND The film has to be finished. Everything depends upon the English insurance company. (*to the French insurance broker*) What does Mr. Johanssen here say?

The French broker[1] *whispers something in the Englishman's ear.*[2]

ENGLISH INSURANCE BROKER (*in English*) It's impossible, I'm sorry, it's impossible. I've been speaking for a whole hour to London to the insurance company. You can't redo the scenes with Alexandre with another actor. I'm sorry. You'll have to find another solution.

FRENCH BROKER (*in French*) Monsieur Johanssen says that he spoke with London for a whole hour last night. The English insurance company says it is out of the question to reshoot Alexandre's scenes with another actor. Therefore, only one solution remains: you must simplify the plot and wind up shooting in five days instead of two weeks as originally planned. If you do that, the insurance company agrees to cover you completely.

BERTRAND (*to* FERRAND) Five days?

FERRAND Five days! We'd have to cut drastically.

FERRAND *goes over to* JOELLE *who has remained sitting in a corner of the screening room during the entire discussion.*

---

1. The role of the French insurance broker is played by Marcel Berbert, the actual executive producer of *Day for Night*.

[2. Although the credits list this role as being played by Henry Graham, the latter is actually a pseudonym for British author Graham Greene, who lives in nearby Antibes and, having met Truffaut at a party during the shooting, agreed to do the role as a lark.]

FERRAND There were some close-ups of Alexandre we were
supposed to take for the fancy-dress sequence. Obviously we'll
have to make do without them.

JOELLE But if that's so, then the scene between Julie and Alphonse with Julie holding the candle won't have any meaning!

FERRAND You know what I think? Why not cut the fancy-dress
sequence entirely? We don't really need it to make the editing
work. The story can very easily be told without it.

JOELLE You're right. It won't even jar the continuity. So then
the only really important scene left with Alexandre in it is the
one where Alphonse kills his father.

FERRAND Instead of setting it in an alley, why not do it in the
heart of the city—say, on the big Parisian square? We can
find some man here in Nice to double for Alexandre.

JOELLE Yes—but even if you use only long shots, the audience
will easily see it's not Alexandre. Unless, of course, Alphonse
shoots him in the back, and we never see his face?

FERRAND Yes, why not? Alphonse will shoot his father in the
back. It might even be more effective that way. It will seem so
much more violent.

JOELLE I've just thought of something else. Why not shoot the
entire sequence with snow on the ground?[1]

[1. "Was the snow at the end of *Meet Pamela* a subtle reference to the
snowy final scenes of *Shoot the Piano Player* and *Fahrenheit 451*?"
(The interviewer could also have included *Mississippi Mermaid* as
well.) Truffaut's answer: "No. It happened just by chance. The role
of JOELLE, the script girl, is based heavily on Suzanne Schiffman,
who has been my assistant and collaborator for fifteen years now. She's
the one who suggested, 'Why not shoot the last scene in the snow?'
I told her, 'Not only that . . . but let's even put your line into the
script!' " (Interview conducted by Claude Beylie in *Ecran 73*, no. 17,
July-August, 1973.)]

Parisian square. Exterior. Day.

Once again there is a great deal of activity on the huge standing set of the Parisian square. A group of firemen from Nice have been called in, and they stand chatting alongside their big red engine.[1] *Upon a signal from the assistant director, the firemen begin to cover the entire square with foam, transforming the sunny Riviera into Parisian winter. The extras swelter in the heat, clothed as they are in furs, heavy coats, rubbers, boots.*

Near the métro entrance FERRAND *and* WALTER *discuss the next shot.*

FERRAND   Track the camera just as you did before . . . but come in closer, much closer, this time when Alphonse walks out of the subway.

WALTER   Yes, that should be better. But there's still the problem with the revolver. The audience has to see it earlier, don't you think?

JOELLE *comes over with a rather tall middle-aged man.*

JOELLE   Ferrand, this is the man who will be doubling for Alexandre.

FERRAND   Oh, yes! How do you do, sir!

Both he and WALTER *examine the man silently.*

FERRAND   Would you mind, monsieur, walking away from us— so we can see better how you'll look? Thank you.

The man moves out of camera range.

WALTER *(quietly)*   The hair's too long at the neck.

FERRAND   We can fix that. Odile! You see that man over there?

[1. The shot of the fire engine, whether intentional or not, is reminiscent of a similar one in *Fahrenheit 451*.]

He's doubling for Alexandre. I'd like you to cut his hair a bit at the neck so he'll resemble him more.

ODILE Of course, sir.

ODILE *rushes off.* BERNARD *arrives, a revolver in hand.*

BERNARD This is the gun you wanted for Alphonse, isn't it?

FERRAND Yes, that's the one I chose. Right.

In another part of the square, the assistant director is giving last minute instructions to the extras.

JEAN-FRANÇOIS Please take your places in the exact spots I indicated earlier. Now, all you people who are to come out of the subway entrance . . .

While the extras scatter about the square, FERRAND *gives a final look over the scene. On the subway steps, armed with a broom,* BERNARD *works hurriedly, spreading out the false snow which seems too piled up in places.*

FERRAND Tell me, Bernard, doesn't this snow bother you a bit? I'm afraid it's going to appear too white, too clean-looking. . . .

BERNARD (*ever the movie buff*) Don't worry. When I get through with it this could pass as a set for *The Snow Was Black!*[1]

At the top of the subway steps FERRAND *bumps into* ALPHONSE, *who is about to take his position down below.*

ALPHONSE I've something I wanted to show you: a telegram I just received from Tokyo. I've been offered a film there. I think I should say yes.

FERRAND (*reading the telegram*) Oh, yes. Turgenev's *First Love.* It's a beautiful story.

ALPHONSE Do you think it might make a good film?[2]

[1. *La Neige Était Sale* ("The Snow Was Black"), a 1952 thriller set in Occupied France and starring Daniel Gélin and Valentine Tessier, was based on the Georges Simenon novel of the same name.]

[2. A film version of *First Love* was made, although not in Japan, in 1970, directed by actor Maximilian Schell. It starred John Moulder Brown and Dominique Sanda as the young lovers. Ironically, the role of the mother was played by Valentina Cortese, ALPHONSE's "mother" in *Meet Pamela*.]

François Truffaut directs Jean-Pierre Léaud.
"People like us are happy only in our work, you must realize that, in our work of making movies . . ."

FERRAND With a Japanese actress in the role of the young girl and you as the Frenchman? Yes, that could work out very well. Yes. Certainly.

ALPHONSE Anyway, I've already decided to say yes, if only because it's being shot in Tokyo—and Tokyo will put twelve thousand miles between me and all my shitty problems!

ALPHONSE *takes out the revolver* BERNARD *gave him earlier. He asks* FERRAND *how he should aim: from the hip or at arm's length.*

FERRAND I like it better held out at arm's length. That way it will stand out more against the snow.

ALPHONSE (*laughing*) Point-blank, huh?

FERRAND Point-blank is it, exactly!

JOELLE *comes over to remind* FERRAND *that* JULIE *and* DOCTOR NELSON *are waiting to say goodbye.*

FERRAND Oh, that's right. They're returning to London?

JOELLE No, they're going to Australia for three weeks to attend a medical congress.

FERRAND Good. I'm on my way! And then, afterward, we'll start shooting, huh?

FERRAND *goes over to kiss* JULIE *and to shake* DOCTOR NELSON's *hand. [This edge of the set, not in use during the sequence, still appears very summery. There is a slight drizzle in the air—which, incidentally, does not match the other shots in the Parisian square.]*

[FERRAND *reminds* JULIE *he will be seeing her in Paris later on when they work on the post-synch.] Then he returns to where the crew are standing, waiting.*

DOCTOR NELSON *has noticed* ALPHONSE, *standing off to one side.* NELSON *whispers something into his wife's ear, and she walks over to* ALPHONSE. ALPHONSE *holds out his hand, rather ceremoniously; but* JULIE, *with a lovely smile, leans forward and kisses him sweetly on the mouth instead.*

JULIE Goodbye, Alphonse.

ALPHONSE Goodbye, Julie.

JULIE Good luck!

Jacqueline Bisset and Jean-Pierre Léaud.

Jean-Pierre Léaud.

ALPHONSE Thanks. You too . . .

JULIE *returns to where* DOCTOR NELSON *stands, waiting. They get into the [little red sports] car and drive off.* JULIE *turns around one last time to wave goodbye to the crew.*

And now FERRAND *begins shooting the last scene of* Meet Pamela. *The camera tracks alongside* ALPHONSE *as he comes up out of the métro station. He takes his revolver from inside his jacket, uncocks it, walking rapidly all the while through the crowd of extras. He stops in the middle of the busy street, aims carefully, fires. Then, upon* FERRAND'S *shouted directions,* AL-PHONSE *turns and runs. The "false Alexandre" falls, sliding down the stone steps between two buildings, only his back visible to the camera.*

The sequence is shot many times, in various manners. As the day wanes, the scene grows increasingly more dramatic. The final take is shot against a completely dark sky.

At last, FERRAND *is satisfied. The shooting of* Meet Pamela *is over.*

The next morning. A bright sunshiny day. The entire crew has gathered just inside the entrance to the Victorine to say goodbye. FERRAND *moves from one little group to another, thanking everyone, making small talk. It is only now that he learns from* ALPHONSE *that the latter will be remaining for a few more days on the Côte d'Azur "to get a good rest." As for* JEAN-FRANÇOIS, *he has a new car waiting for him in Paris, courtesy of the production department, to take the place of the one that went careening down into the ravine—but the question now is how to get back to the capital city as cheaply as possible. He asks* BERNARD *for a lift in his station wagon; but* BERNARD, *independent as ever, refuses.* BERNARD *still believes in traveling alone.*

FERRAND *also learns that the young assistant cameraman is taking* ODILE *to meet his parents.*

ODILE [*sitting happily on her fiancé's motorcycle as they prepare to take off*]: We're going to be married!

FERRAND Well, that's a surprise! You certainly hid things well enough, the two of you! I'm sure none of the crew even suspected it.

ASSISTANT CAMERAMAN　Yes. Well—you see, Odile's known a lot of men, and I've known very few women. So it kind of averages out, don't you think?

FERRAND　Perfectly! I wish you both much happiness. Congratulations!

FERRAND *leaves them to make his farewell with* WALTER.

FERRAND　So long, Walter.

WALTER　So long, Ferrand.

FERRAND　Oh—and many thanks! The photography of the film is exceptional. I'm very happy.

WALTER　If you're happy, then I'm happy.

FERRAND *is suddenly collared by the same television announcer who was present on the first day of shooting. He is once more surrounded by his own tiny crew.*

ANNOUNCER　Monsieur Ferrand, could you say a few words to our viewers about Alexandre?

FERRAND　No, sorry, but that's too personal—considering the circumstances. Why don't you ask Bertrand, our producer?

ANNOUNCER　I did. He refused.

FERRAND　How about Alphonse?

ANNOUNCER　Him too. He says he doesn't want to talk about death.

FERRAND　I'm sorry, but it's too special. . . .

FERRAND *rushes off. The announcer looks dumbfounded at his crew.*

ANNOUNCER　What do you know, I've no one to talk to!

All at once, BERNARD *comes over. He strikes a pose before the TV camera.*

BERNARD　I'm still here!

The announcer asks one of his assistants who in hell can this character be, and the man mutters something about the production prop man. The announcer decides it's better than nothing.

ANNOUNCER Tell me, it couldn't have been easy shooting this movie, could it? I've heard rumors about all sorts of strange happenings. Things weren't exactly rosy some days, were they?

BERNARD Not at all, not at all! Everything went perfectly. And, what's more, we hope the public will have as much fun watching this movie as we all had making it!

[BERNARD's *face moves closer to the camera. We realize that he is indeed talking to all of us in the audience . . . not only about* Meet Pamela, *but about* Day for Night *as well.*]

This time the shooting is definitely over. Cars and motorcycles speed out of the tall white gates of the Victorine in all directions. The huge standing set of the Parisian square is empty, more than slightly outrageous-looking, flapping in the wind, surrounded by the palm trees of Nice.

[*The final credits unfold over various helicopter shots of the Victorine: shots of the crew saying their goodbyes, getting into their automobiles, shots of the Parisian square seen from different angles as the helicopter moves in closer and closer, circling round and round. Oval insets of all the leading players appear superimposed over the helicopter shots, beginning with* Jacqueline Bisset. *In each of these the character is seen talking animatedly to someone off-camera—except for* David Markham *as* DOCTOR NELSON, *who is seen listening (the shot having been taken from his scene with* Jean-Pierre Aumont *as they drive to the Nice Airport) and eventually speaking a few words. The Vivaldi-like theme connected with "shooting the film" rises to a crescendo which seems to coincide with the rising of the helicopter which, on the last notes of music, has pulled away from the Victorine completely to let us have a view of the city beyond.*]

François Truffaut.
Cinema in action.

Selected List of Grove Press Drama and Theater Paperbacks

E312   ARDEN, JOHN / Serjeant Musgrave's Dance / $2.45 [See also Modern British Drama, Henry Popkin, ed. GT614 / $5.95]

B109   ARDEN, JOHN / Three Plays: Live Like Pigs, The Waters of Babylon, The Happy Haven / $2.45

E127   ARTAUD, ANTONIN / The Theater and Its Double (Critical Study) / $2.95

E425   BARAKA, IMAMU AMIRI (LEROI JONES) / The Baptism and The Toilet / $2.45

E540   BARNES, PETER / The Ruling Class / $2.95

E471   BECKETT, SAMUEL / Cascando and Other Short Dramatic Pieces (Words and Music, Film, Play, Come and Go, Eh Joe, Endgame) / $1.95

E96   BECKETT, SAMUEL / Endgame / $1.95

E318   BECKETT, SAMUEL / Happy Days / $2.45

E226   BECKETT, SAMUEL / Krapp's Last Tape, plus All That Fall, Embers, Act Without Words I and II / $2.45

E33   BECKETT, SAMUEL / Waiting For Godot / $1.95 [See also Seven Plays of the Modern Theater, Harold Clurman, ed. GT422 / $4.95]

B79   BEHAN, BRENDAN / The Quare Fellow* and The Hostage**: Two Plays / $2.45 *[See also Seven Plays of the Modern Theater, Harold Clurman, ed. GT422 / $4.95] **[See also Modern British Drama, Henry Popkin, ed. GT614 / $5.95]

B117   BRECHT, BERTOLT / The Good Woman of Setzuan / $1.95

B80   BRECHT, BERTOLT / The Jewish Wife and Other Short Plays (In Search of Justice, The Informer, The Elephant Calf, The Measures Taken, The Exception and the Rule, Salzburg Dance of Death) / $1.65

B90   BRECHT, BERTOLT / The Mother / $1.45

B108   BRECHT, BERTOLT / Mother Courage and Her Children / $1.50

B333   BRECHT, BERTOLT / The Threepenny Opera / $1.45

B88   BRECHT, BERTOLT / The Visions of Simone Machard / $1.25

E517   BULGAKOV, MIKHAIL / Flight: A Play in Eight Dreams and Four Acts / $2.25

GT422 CLURMAN, HAROLD (Ed.) / Seven Plays of the Modern Theater / $4.95 (Waiting For Godot by Samuel Beckett, The Quare Fellow by Brendan Behan, A Taste of Honey by Shelagh Delaney, The Connection by Jack Gelber, The Balcony by Jean Genet, Rhinoceros by Eugene Ionesco, and The Birthday Party by Harold Pinter)

E159   DELANEY, SHELAGH / A Taste of Honey / $1.95 (See also Modern British Drama, Henry Popkin, ed., GT614 / $5.95, and Seven Plays of the Modern Theater, Harold Clurman, ed. GT422 / $4.95)

E402   DURRENMATT, FRIEDRICH / An Angel Comes to Babylon and Romulus the Great / $3.95

E612   DURRENMATT, FRIEDRICH / Play Strindberg / $1.95

E344   DURRENMATT, FRIEDRICH / The Visit / $2.75

E223   GELBER, JACK / The Connection / $2.45 [See also Seven Plays of the Modern Theater, Harold Clurman, ed. GT422 / $4.95]

E130   GENET, JEAN / The Balcony / $2.95 [See also Seven Plays of the Modern Theater, Harold Clurman, ed. GT422 / $4.95]

E208   GENET, JEAN / The Blacks: A Clown Show / $2.95

E577   GENET, JEAN / The Maids and Deathwatch: Two Plays / $2.95

E374   GENET, JEAN / The Screens / $1.95

E457   HERBERT, JOHN / Fortune and Men's Eyes / $2.95

B154   HOCHHUTH, ROLF / The Deputy / $2.95

E456   IONESCO, EUGENE / Exit the King / $2.95

E101   IONESCO, EUGENE / Four Plays (The Bald Soprano, The Lesson, The Chairs,* Jack, or The Submission) / $1.95 *[See also Eleven Short Plays of the Modern Theater, Samuel Moon, ed. B107 / $2.45]

E646   IONESCO, EUGENE / A Hell of a Mess / $3.95

E506   IONESCO, EUGENE / Hunger and Thirst and Other Plays / $1.95

E189   IONESCO, EUGENE / The Killer and Other Plays (Improvisation, or The Shepherd's Chameleon, Maid to Marry) / $2.45

E613   IONESCO, EUGENE / Killing Game / $1.95

E259   IONESCO, EUGENE / Rhinoceros* and Other Plays (The Leader, The Future is in Eggs, or It Takes All Sorts to Make a World) / $1.95 *[See also Seven Plays of the Modern Theater, Harold Clurman, ed. GT422 / $4.95]

E485   IONESCO, EUGENE / A Stroll in the Air and Frenzy for Two: Two Plays / $2.45

E119   IONESCO, EUGENE / Three Plays (Amédée, The New Tenant, Victims of Duty) / $2.95

E387   IONESCO, EUGENE / Notes and Counter Notes / $3.95

E633   LAHR, JOHN (Ed.) / Grove Press Modern Drama / $6.95 (The Caucasian Chalk Circle by Bertolt Brecht, The Toilet by Imamu Amiri Baraka (LeRoi Jones), The White House Murder Case by Jules Feiffer, The Blacks by Jean Genet, Rhinoceros by Eugene Ionesco, Tango by Slawomir Mrozek)

E433   MROZEK, SLAWOMIR / Tango / $1.95

E462   NICHOLS, PETER / Joe Egg / $2.95

E567   ORTON, JOE / What The Butler Saw / $2.40

E583   OSBORNE, JOHN / Inadmissible Evidence / $2.45

B354   PINTER, HAROLD / Old Times / $1.95

E315   PINTER, HAROLD / The Birthday Party* and The Room: Two Plays / $1.95 *[See also Seven Plays of the Modern Theater, Harold Clurman, ed. GT422 / $4.95]

E299   PINTER, HAROLD / The Caretaker* and The Dumb Waiter: Two Plays / $1.95 *[See also Modern British Drama, Henry Popkin, ed. GT422 / $5.95]

E411   PINTER, HAROLD / The Homecoming / $1.95

E432   PINTER, HAROLD / The Lover, Tea Party, The Basement: Three Plays / $1.95

E480   PINTER, HAROLD / A Night Out, Night School, Revue Sketches: Early Plays / $1.95

GT614   POPKIN, HENRY (Ed.) / Modern British Drama / $5.95 (A Taste of Honey by Shelagh Delaney, The Hostage by Brendan Behan, Roots by Arnold Wesker, Serjeant Musgrave's Dance by John Arden, One Way Pendulum by N. F. Simpson, The Caretaker by Harold Pinter)

E635   SHEPARD, SAM / The Tooth of Crime and Geography of a Horsedreamer / $3.95

E626   STOPPARD, TOM / Jumpers / $1.95

B319   STOPPARD, TOM / Rosencrantz and Guilderstern Are Dead / $1.95

E660   STOREY, DAVID / In Celebration / $2.95